Greg Gilbert
1125 Highway 195 S.
Washington, AR 71862
Greg@GregLGilbert.com
GregLGilbert.com

The
"Power Of Better!"
Series

Volume I

Leading Like You Own It!
Why We Never Wax A Rental Car.

by Greg Gilbert

Disclaimer

This book is designed to provide information on leadership. This information is provided and sold with the knowledge that the publisher and author do not offer any legal or other professional advice. In the case of a need for any such expertise consult with the appropriate professional.

This book does not contain all information available on the subject. This book has not been created to be specific to any individual's or organizations' situation or needs. Every effort has been made to make this book as accurate as possible. However, there may be typographical and or content errors. Therefore, this book should serve only as a general guide and not as the ultimate source of subject information.

This book contains information that might be dated and is intended only to educate. The author and publisher shall have no liability or responsibility to any person or entity regarding any loss or damage incurred, or alleged to have incurred, directly or indirectly, by the information contained in this book.

Copyright

Copyright © 2015 by Greg Gilbert

All rights reserved. No part of this publication may be reproduced, distributed, or transmitted in any form or by any means, including photocopying, recording, or other electronic or mechanical methods, without the prior written permission of the author, except in the case of brief quotations embodied in critical reviews and certain other noncommercial uses permitted by copyright law. For permission requests, write to the author, addressed "Attention: Permissions Requested," at the address below.

At Last Light Publishing
1125 Highway 195 South
Washington, Arkansas 71862
870 777-1454

Ordering Information:

Quantity sales. Special discounts are available on quantity purchases by corporations, associations, and others. For details, contact the author at the address above or by E-mail at Sandy@GregLGilbert.com

"There's an app for that."® - Steve Jobs

"There's a chapter for that." - Greg Gilbert

"If you are a Manager, Supervisor or HR Manager, this book contains a chapter for what you've been through, going through or headed for." -Greg Gilbert- Author of "The Power Of Better - Leading Like You Own It! - Leadership Guide for Managers, Supervisors and HR Managers.

What Others Are Saying;

The message in what you are about to read has been presented to hundreds of audiences with thousands of attendees. This is what they are saying;

I first had the privilege of hearing Greg speak during a seminar in Little Rock and immediately I knew I would be doing a disservice to my employees if I did not share with them the message he delivers. Greg brings to the table tremendous insight about leadership, relationships and personal responsibilities that demands one to take their personal inventory; but he does it with such a humorous gentleness that you're left with a feeling of, "Wow! I can't wait to get started!"

We invited Greg to speak at our Leadership Retreat in July. Sixteen (out of seventeen) of our returned evaluation questionnaires had a positive comment regarding Greg. (The one without a positive comment, did not have any comments.) Here are a few examples, "[Greg Gilbert] changed my life! He is an amazing speaker and has a wealth of valuable information." "Best speaker I've ever heard!" And "The most helpful aspects of the retreat were Greg. He was very interesting and gave me things to think about and use." One of the questions on the questionnaire was "What aspects of the retreat did you like best?" Ten of the sixteen answered that Greg's presentation was the best.

Thank you Greg. As one person wrote, [your presentation] "is from the heart".

-L. Hanson, – Rogers, Arkansas

"A few hours after attending your program, I was one of many first responders to the tragic death of a young teenager in my community. That's when some of the lessons you shared that morning, really hit home. Your program is about more than leadership; it is also about life. I wanted to personally share what they meant to me that night."
- J. Hollis to Greg Gilbert on March 13, 2014

Greg,
Feedback from attendees has been more than positive! Your approach was on target, our staff shared that they appreciated the fact that you weren't "telling" us how to do things, but shared ideas, experience & rationale for these approaches. I'll let you know how we progress. Take care,
J. Bueg, PHR
Harrison, AR 72602

"Your program was very pertinent and useful. Your "real life" stories allowed you to make a connection with your audience." – R. Davis – CFO, Paragould Light Water & Cable

----

E-mail to Little Rock meeting planner:

I didn't tell you how much I enjoyed the meeting yesterday.
The location was absolutely perfect….what a great idea to use that facility!
And the program you all put together for us was just what I needed to hear.
The student choir reminded us of our mission at the health dept; to create a better world for them.

But by far, the guitar HR speaker really brought home important messages to me personally AND professionally.

Please tell all your team members that we all appreciate the hard work that went into planning and implementing such a good program for us.

"Greg, I want to thank you again for the outstanding session you conducted. Our supervisors and manager walked away with more than they were expecting. Keep it up....you are a valuable asset to the HR field." – V. Kieth –
Human Resources Manager – Longview, TX

"This is the best seminar I have ever attended. Very relatable and useful. Not all about rules and laws but relationships. Thank you, truly thank you. You are an inspiration." – KT – Absolute Care Management – 2-12-13

Leadership impacting right when I needed it. – KK – HR Mgr. Startek

----

"I have attended several leadership classes and left without anything to challenge me as a supervisor. This format and presentation was very beneficial and I plan on reviewing all of the material again as I strive to become a more effective and efficient manager." – WC- Resident Engineer – Arkansas Highway Transportation Department

----

"Plenty of information provided in a basic and fundamental manner. Great job!" – KWJ-Section Head-Safety and Training- Arkansas Highway Transportation Department

----

"Our company allowed us the opportunity to work with Greg on a one-on-one basis. The experience was awesome and the training that he shared was very educational and personal. I walked away with some great learning tools. I would recommend his leadership course to anyone. My mission is; honesty and integrity and to always remain thankful." – P.E. Acct. Exec. – Express Personnel Services

----

The format of real life experiences left more of an impact than the normal classroom "do this and don't do this" approach." – SM- Arkansas Highway Transportation Department

----

"I think you did a great job. You are a great orator. Learned things about myself I need to improve on. I thought it was very educational; enough to have you give a presentation to everyone in our office." – EC- Assistant General Manager – Express Personnel Services

----

"Your presentation was loved by our entire group. Everyone commented on how funny you are but how important your message is as well especially since we all get so caught up in our busy schedules. You helped remind us about what is important in life and gave us some good people management tools as well. You certainly helped to liven up a day full of legal regulations and laws and that is not easy to do!"
M. H. – President RRVHR Association

"We truly enjoyed your presentation. The message was one for not only Human Resource professionals but for every walk of life. I was inspired by your outlook and reminded that life is what I intend to make of it. This was an important message for me and I am sure it touched many others. I believe that every person we come in contact with plays an important role for one, if not both people."
Thank you again,
Courtney – HR Conference Coordinator

"What a wonderful presentation you made for our Arkansas Transit Association 25th anniversary. Our members enjoyed your stories and I think all of us deal with many of the same issues every day. Thank you for joining us and sharing your presentation."
Ann-Arkansas Transit Association

"We gave them an evaluation sheet to hand in at the end of the training and you were on it. All the evaluations I have read, gave you good and very good marks. Not one bad mark. I will let others know about you and hopefully have you back another time. Thank you again for your passion for what you do, it was very uplifting to many."
KH-Families & Children Together, Inc. (South Central Arkansas Head Start/EHS/ABC Programs)

"Thank you. You have opened my eyes to the true importance of what I do as a supervisor. Your real life stories presented leadership in a manner where I "get it". I see where I've dropped the ball." - Comment to Greg Gilbert at the end of a Little Rock, AR program.

"What I enjoyed most about his seminar is that he is not just a speaker or instructor delivering someone else's material. He shared personally witnessed successes and failures and what led to each. All managers and supervisors can relate to and learn from this seminar." – Comment from a Lebanon, Pennsylvania seminar attendee to their HR Manager

Table Of Contents

Acknowledgments - Page 18

Introduction - Page 22

Chapter 1.- Nothing Changes Until Something Is Written! - Page 29

Chapter 2.- What Has Improved As A Result Of Your Actions? - Page 31

Chapter 3.- The Unwritten, Unspoken, But Fully Implemented Memo That Could Be Slowly Killing Your Business! - Page 33

Chapter 4.- The Success Formula Of Education, Engagement and Accountability. - Page 37

Chapter 5.- Bring Back The Tight Ship! - Page 41

Chapter 6.- The Benefit Of "Leading Like You Own It!" - Page 42

Chapter 7.- Have Any Great Supervisors, Managers or Leaders Been Born In Your Company? - Page 46

Chapter 8.- Your Very Own Widget Factory. - Page 48

Chapter 9.- The RIPM. (Retired In Place Manager) - Page 50

Chapter 10.- You Have A Team, Be A Coach! - Page 54

Chapter 11.- The Greatest Bang For Your Time. - Page 55

Chapter 12.- Put Me On Discipline. Please! Page 56

Chapter 13.- Never Assume! ALWAYS Clarify! Page 58

Chapter 14.- Your Influence Goes Deeper Than An Org Chart - Page 62

Chapter 15.- They Don't pay Me What I'm Worth - Page 64

Chapter 16.- Seniority Vs. Results - Who Wins? - Page 66

Chapter 17.- Honesty And Integrity - Page 69

Chapter 18.- You Are The Difference - Page 70

Chapter 19.- The Leadership Tool Kit - Page 72

Chapter 20.- Two High And Two Low - Page 74

Chapter 21.- I Would Have Done A Better Job If I'd Known We Were Going To Lay People Off! - Page 75

Chapter 22.- Attendance - I Need You At Work And On Time. Enough Said! - Page 77

Chapter 23.- Are You For Me? - Page 81

Chapter 24.- Trust, Guts And The Benefit Of Both! - Page 83

Chapter 25.- Whenever Money or Time Is Invested, There Are Expectations! - Page 89

Chapter 26.- Not On My Watch! - Page 91

Chapter 27.- Dear Boss, - Page 95

Chapter 28.- We Need To Be Quicker In Growing Tired Of The Attack. - Page 98

Chapter 29.- Growing Tired Of The Attack. Part Two. - Page 102

Chapter 30.- I've Talked To Him Eight Times - Let's Fire Him - Page 104

Chapter 31.- GPS In The Company Vehicle, Friend Or Foe? You Get To Choose! - Page 107

Chapter 32.- Show me on paper what you are doing to improve your team. - Page 113

Chapter 33.- How To Poorly Impersonate A Supervisor. - Page 115

Chapter 34.- How To Fix Most Performance Problems. - Page 120

Chapter 35.- We Are Government! We Are Different! - Page 122

Chapter 36.- Your First Leader - Page 125

Chapter 37.- What Culture Is In Your Wallet? (The Poker Game) - Page 128

Chapter 38.- The Line In The Sand. - Page 131

Chapter 39.- Why Do You Do What You Do? - Page 133

Chapter 40.- The Bucket Story - Page 137

Chapter 41.- My Greatest HR Challenge! - Page 141

Chapter 42.- Find A Way To Say Yes To Your Customers. - Page 144

Chapter 43.- Buy The Blanked De Blank Roses! - Page 146

Chapter 44.- Would You Buy Your Team With You As The Leader? - Page 148

Chapter 45.- We Can't Come Over, Our Weed Eater Is Broken! - Page 149

Chapter 46.- Pot Roast And Southwestern Bell - Page 150

Chapter 47.- Bob's Rules. - Page 151

Chapter 48.- Leadership Lessons From David Allen Coe - Page 152

Chapter 49.- Was The Title "Lying Leadership" Already Taken? - Page 155

Chapter 50.- Now; It's Your Turn To Appraise Me. - Page 159

Chapter 51.- Help! I Work For An Electric Boss. - Page 161

Chapter 52.- Pool Hall Leadership Lessons - Page 163

Chapter 53.- Lead Or Exit - A Coaching Lesson In Football, Business And Government! - Page 166

Chapter 54.- Welcome Aboard. Is It Okay If I Call You At-Will? - Page 170

Chapter 55.- Leadership And Life Lessons I Learned From My Guitar! - Page 174

Chapter 56.- Daily Task List Readjustment, Cancer, Perspective and What Matters Is Measured! - Page 175

Chapter 57.- I'll Learn Your Name If You Are Still Here In Six Months! - Page 178

Chapter 58.- What 90% Of Managers Won't Do And How That Can Affect Your Income! - Page 180

Chapter 59.- Learning From Our Mistakes. - Page 182

Chapter 60.- Where Is A Leader When You Need One? - Page 185

Chapter 61.- Pick Your Battles And Never Miss A Good Opportunity To Shut Up! - Page 188

Chapter 62.- There May Be Only One Boss Like This But They Move Around A Lot. - Page 191

Chapter 63.- The Layoff Prevention Plan- Page 193

Chapter 64.- I'm Going To Tell You Something But- Page 194

Chapter 65.- We Will Always Beat Me. - Page 197

Chapter 66.- Feedback! Always Sought, Seldom Found! - Page 198

Chapter 67.- Papaw, When Will Spider-Man Stop Growing? - Page 200

Chapter 68.- The Life Saving Value Of Education. - Page 202

Chapter 69.- You May Only Get One Opportunity To Say Or Do The Right Thing! - Page 204

Chapter 70.- Life Will Give You TMO's (Teaching Moment Opportunities). Don't Blow Them! - Page 207

Chapter 71.- Losing Your Barbara Will Cost You Thousands! - Page 210

Chapter 72.- Where Are The Worms and Good Team Members? - Page 212

Chapter 73.- It Will Be A Long Uphill Battle If Fun Is Not Included! - Page 215

Chapter 74.- Are You Closing Your Gap? - Page 217

Chapter 75.- Tale Of Two Pities - Page 218

Chapter 76.- Danger! Selfish Or Selfless Choice Ahead! - Page 220

Chapter 77.- Are You A Settler? - Page 222

Chapter 78.- Slow Down. You're Making Me Look Bad. - Page 224

Chapter 79.- You Are A Professional. Be Proud Of It! - Page 225

Chapter 80.- Why? It's Not Your Money. - Page 226

Chapter 81.- Who Owns Your Company? - Page 227

Chapter 82.- There Are No "Just A" Positions Here- Page 230

Chapter 83.- I Can Resist Everything But Temptation. - RIP - Ken Langston- Page 230

Chapter 84.- Be A William. - Page 232

The Final chapter. - The True Power Of Better! - Page 234

Epilogue - Page 237

Thank You! - Page 241

About Greg Gilbert- Page 242

Acknowledgments

There is no way I could list all the great leaders and mentors that have influenced this book. I would certainly leave someone out.

However, I did find a list of initials on a thank you page on my first website in 2004. My memory was probably better then than it is now, so they will be at the bottom of the page.

I want to thank my first leaders, my parents, Thomas and Virginia Gilbert. Thank you for teaching me and a big thank you for moving our family to the farm. I learned about work ethic, urgency, preventive maintenance, how to build and fix things, care, compassion and many other things that helped me in leadership and life.

The time spent and lessons learned in our barn/shop have been invaluable. Where else would a fourteen-year-old get the knowledge, courage and support to totally tear a Suzuki 50 motorcycle apart to replace high gear?

If I had to rank the importance of my education, it would be my years in Human Resources first. My years on the farm second. My years in a classroom third and every other educational experience after that.

The next acknowledgment goes to Sandy, my wife of nearly 40 years. She has followed me through three corners and the middle of Arkansas after my job turned into a career. She has also supported me through every lesson contained in this book.

She has always been a great sounding board for a guy that wakes up every day with new thoughts and ideas; some are good, some are bad. She has this unique way of letting me down easily without damaging my confidence or creativity. She and I both know there will be new ideas tomorrow.

I want to acknowledge the two greatest daughters a dad could have; my favorite oldest daughter, Amber and my favorite youngest daughter, Autumn. It is so rewarding to watch you grow and develop into wonderful adults. I'm so thankful I had the opportunity to help. You made me more responsible and accountable. I look forward to making more memories.

My two grandsons, Kel and Kasen. I never knew papawing could be so much fun. My goal is to make as many memories with you and the rest of our family as possible.

The corporate attorney that instilled the fear of "if it's not written, it didn't occur" in me in 1978. That began this "journey through my journal." That journey is what you have in your hands and the presentations that have been heard by thousands.

Tom Green. I want to thank you for giving me the opportunity to serve as your "Personnel Manager". This book nor the person I am today would not exist without that opportunity and the twelve years that followed.

Charles Gowder. Thank you for pulling me from retirement. Thank you for calling me when I was out standing in my field. Yes, I was out standing in my field with the cows. Thank you for asking me to design a management development course that was not smoke and mirrors, dog and pony show, left brain, right brain or personality profiles. Thank you for asking me to design a course that would help managers produce excellent results through others. This book would not exist without that request.

Perry Buster, RIP and thank you. Perry taught Sandy and I to play guitar when we were 50 years old. He had us making noise that sounded enough like music to keep us interested. I've always been good at poetry and rhyme, but I never had the ability to put it in a song until Perry came along.

I thank Perry for the enjoyment of crafting a song from an inspiration, the emotional feedback from someone hearing one of my songs, a song honoring veterans on Arkansas' largest ABC affiliate and the laughter with "Mr. HR With A Guitar". None of this would have been possible without Perry.

There are so many more leaders, mentors, speakers, authors and friends that have influenced my life and this book. I am appreciative for all the paths that I have crossed in my life and career. Some paths were pleasurable, some painful, but I learned from both.

If our paths have crossed or if they do cross in the future, I hope the experience is pleasurable.

Now for those initials of leaders and mentors that were on my thank you page in 2004;

Here we go,

Thank you, G, TG, MG, TG, WG, TB, BR, PC, MC, JA, HM, CC, JF, SG, PS, JV, DB, GH, SK, DG, JP, MHJ, LL, AG, BH, PH, JC, KB, SB, MH, MR, LD, JA, DC, AG, CG, CG, LN, BF, RH, DR, FH, TG, RM, TRG, JM, HC, JD, AD, JH, MF, CY, KF, JD, PA, FB, RA, JM, BN, KH, RY, PH, MM, MG, BH, FT, JA, GK, JH, JB, SL, RF, MM, SM, DP, DW, LB, DM, RJ, MG, AE, KG, GM, JR, ZZ, WJ, LW, JM, CW, SW, BW, LM, DM, LW, DL, AC, RF, MP, JP, DP, DG, MV, BG.

I may have forgotten some, but you get the picture. I didn't do it on my own, neither should you or your leadership team.

Introduction -

The "The Power Of Better!" Series

Volume I

Leading Like You Own It!

Why We Never Wax A Rental Car.

I believe the best way we can begin is to see if we are on the same page, book, library or planet concerning leadership. Below are a few of my core beliefs that make up my presentations and this book:

I believe "due to the economy" is frequently used in error because it sounds better than "due to poor leadership."

I believe in Education, Engagement and total Accountability of every team member at every level.

I believe businesses succeed or fail because of the presence or absence of Education, Engagement and Accountability.

I believe the results, profitability and morale of any organization can be improved by increasing Education, Engagement and Accountability.
I believe it is impossible to lose Hope when we are getting better at something.

I believe in having FUN! "Mr. HR With A Guitar" was created to add humor and a unique method of Education to my presentations.

I believe high expectations should accompany every expense. A paycheck is an expense. Organizations succeed or fail because of the level of expectations.

I believe team members have high expectations also. These expectations are normally met through Education, Engagement and Accountability. When the high expectations of an employer and employee are both met, success is guaranteed.

I believe that a "high on trust, low on rules" organization will ALWAYS outperform a "high on rules, low on trust" organization.

I believe the highest performing teams have leaders they know are "For Them." The teams that struggle with poor results and morale have leaders they believe are "Against Them" or "For Themselves."

I believe too many managers and supervisors have more leadership tools and authority than they have confidence and guts to use.

I believe great doctors save lives. I also believe great Managers, Supervisors and HR Managers save livelihoods, change lives and impact families.

I believe Managers, Supervisors and HR Managers are Professionals and should view themselves as such.

I believe in the role of coaching. The origin of the word "coach" was to get you from where you are to where you need to be (as in Stage Coach, flying Coach or motor coach). Great Managers, Supervisors and HR Managers are great Coaches.

I believe in constant improvement. Managers manage, Supervisors supervise, but true leaders improve. Distributing tasks, putting out fires and maintaining puts livelihoods in jeopardy.

I believe in personal and professional development. My development should NEVER be the total responsibility of my employer.

Most importantly, I believe this book can help your organization.

If we are even close to being on the same page, let's get started.

We've all seen the question; If you could have lunch with any three people, dead or alive, who would you choose?

There are two different directions we can take with our answer. We will either make emotional or educational selections. It depends on whether you want a hug or help. Some choices may provide both.

This book is a leadership lunch with hundreds of years of my leaders and mentors experience.

I also consider this book a "Leadership In The Round". Let me explain. Although I believe leadership coaching is where I can make my greatest contribution, I also enjoy songwriting. One of my songs was featured as a Veteran's Day Tribute on our largest ABC affiliate in Arkansas.

My most inspirational songwriting lessons have occurred at the Bluebird Cafe in Nashville, Tennessee. They have songwriters in the round nearly every night.

There are three or four big name country songwriters taking turns sharing one of their hits. They share the inspiration and the process that led to the success of the song. Many times there is a co-writer. They may not be present, but their assistance is always acknowledged. Every time I attend the Bluebird, I am inspired to come home and write a song.

This book will be your "Leadership In The Round". Instead of songwriters, you have access to hundreds of years of my leaders and my mentors experience. Just as some songs have a co-writer, this book has many co-writers in the form of my leaders, their leaders, my mentors and their mentors. The ripple effects are endless. You have the opportunity to pass these batons to others.

I never left the Bluebird without writing a song. I hope you never pick up this book without implementing a positive change in your Leadership or Life.

This book was written to inspire and encourage you to become a better leader by using every leadership tool available.

Making the decision to become a better leader is similar to making the decision to quit smoking or lose weight. Something will trigger the personal inspiration to make the necessary changes. I hope this book can serve as that trigger.

No one can convince or shame you into this decision. You must see the long-term value and make the decision on your own.

However, there is another similarity between these decisions. Sometimes there is a significant health event that strongly encourages you to expedite the weight loss or smoking cessation.

A significant life event could also occur as a result of not applying basic leadership principles.

These significant health and life events are minimized by "getting better" now; not later.

Q. How are you doing?
A. I'm getting better.

Over the past ten years, I have shared with thousands how to handle different situations. These situations have varied from crying employees to poor performers to improving team members to how to challenge and reward consistent high performers.

I spent my last 12 years prior to retirement as the primary Human Resources contact for over 2200 team members. Each phone call was a lesson in how to handle different and sometimes difficult situations.

However, none of this prepared me for how to handle a personal diagnosis of cancer in 2014. There is no training for this. I am very happy to say that after six months, three hospital visits, four surgeries and plenty of prayers, I am cancer free. The doctor says the cancer is in remission. I prefer cancer free. But this is not a book about cancer or illness. This is a book about getting better in different aspects of Leadership and Life.

The most commonly asked question during my illnesses was "How are you doing?" Fortunately, I was able to give the answer that contains the most Hope; "I'm getting better."

I am very aware that some cancer patients are never again able to say those words. I am humbled and grateful to be "better." But again, this is not a book about illness or cancer, it is about getting better in Leadership and Life. Answering this question hundreds of times made me see the joy, encouragement, inspiration, and Hope contained in the words, "I'm getting better."

This book is a collection of personally witnessed tools, lessons and opportunities to become a better Manager, Supervisor, or HR Manager. You are welcome to pick a few and begin the process of getting better, or you can pick just one. Document and track your progress. You MUST be intentional. You will be amazed at the personal pride and satisfaction that always accompany "getting better."

The importance of "getting better" while I can, became very evident during this health challenge. Many of us waste years maintaining when we could be "getting better" on different aspects of Leadership and Life.

I'm inviting you to join me in "The Power Of Better" movement. Improvement, growth and development should be exciting to all of us. I can't imagine a high performer ever being in the maintenance mode.

I hope these lessons save you pain, time and expense in leadership and life. Most of all, I hope these lessons save livelihoods. Doctors may save lives, but leaders have the ability to save livelihoods.

I have created a leadership book that can serve as a reference guide throughout your life. I wrote this so my two daughters, grandkids and you can learn from me, my leaders, mentors and become a better leader in your life. If certain lessons hit home, let me know. Email me at Greg@GregLGilbert.com

This book can also be a guide for numerous leadership meeting discussions.

If you like what you read and would like a program for your organization or group, visit our website at GregLGilbert.com for more information.

Welcome to "The Power Of Better!"

Thank you for your most valuable asset, your time.

Greg Gilbert

Chief Betterment Officer

Greg Gilbert Coaching

Greg@GregLGilbert.com   www.GregLGilbert.com

Chapter 1. Nothing Changes Until Something Is Written!

This book will contain many tools, lessons and opportunities for you to improve in Leadership and Life. Many of these will hit home, step on your toes, grab your shoulders and shake you. However, these will only occur if you give a flip. If you don't give a flip and are in a leadership role, I beg of you, resign. Today. You are putting livelihoods in jeopardy.

Here is a job aid for this book. Copy this page or write this and place it inside the book.

I commit to get better at

_____
_____
_____
_____.

The item(s) you pick may change throughout the book. All I ask is that you pick one item, but you are welcome to be an over-achiever and pick two or more.

If you give a big flip, pick one for the commitment below and discuss it at your next meeting.

My organization could get better at

_____
_____
_____
_____.

You MUST write something. It must be tracked and intentional. This is the first step to the true power of better.

Take Care. NO. Forget that. Take Control.
Greg Gilbert

Chapter 2. What Has Improved As A Result Of Your Actions?

Quick; put down the book. Write two items that have improved in your leadership and/or life in the last year as a direct result of your actions.

Okay, is that completed? Yeah, right. I've asked thousands in my programs to write those two items, and I've only seen one pen hit the paper. Yes, one. I look at their "deer in the headlights" stare for 8-10 seconds and then say stop; you don't have to do that. You can hear and feel the relief return to the room.

Why should that be a difficult request? I can never say this with a straight face, and now I have discovered, I can't even type it without laughing. When you were promoted or brought on board, did they welcome you and say, "we want you to help us keep it just like it is?" NO. They want you to help the organization grow and improve. They want things to "get better."

You can separate yourself from the average and mediocre by always having at least two items you are intentionally improving. Improvement does not occur by accident. The Power Of Better increases your awareness of improvement so you can easily document these two improvements.

Leaders intentional about improvement can quickly answer that question. They protect livelihoods. RIPM (Retired In Place Managers) and managers allowed to maintain, struggle with this question. They place livelihoods in jeopardy. No one is placed in a position of leadership to "keep things as they are".

"The Power Of Better" will provide tools, lessons and the opportunity to become "Better" in different aspects of Leadership and Life. When leaders become "Better", organizations become "Better".

Chapter 3. The Unwritten, Unspoken, But Fully Implemented Memo That Could Be Slowly Killing Your Business!

I want to use this chapter to set the stage for my total belief in Education, Engagement and Accountability.

With some of the survey answers I've received from team members of different companies, I have recognized a problem. Many managers complain about no support on discipline. They complain about not being given the authority to use every one of the leadership tools available. We need to bring this out in the open. These non supportive bosses must be identified, trained or removed.

There is a lack of education, development, team engagement and accountability in some organizations. It is like this unspoken, unwritten memo has gone out to all team members (wink-wink). I believe in full disclosure. I have created a template for these organizations to copy and paste to their letterhead. Let's go ahead and clear the air.

To: All Team Members

From: Upper-level boss/employee mindsets

1. Effective immediately, all formal and informal training will be stopped. Although there has been no developmental training in years, we wanted to remove any glimmer of hope that we are interested in your success. In the past, we had used the excuse of tight budgets when we just didn't want to spend the time, money or effort on you.

We have chosen more of a "maintaining" approach instead of improvement. We consider team development an expense with no return on investment. This is especially true when no one is ever held accountable. (See item 3 below.) We have decided to discontinue our effort of acting like we want to develop and invest in our team members.

We will equip you to do your job, and any extra developmental training will be at your cost on your time. If the company or the customers benefit from your personal development, we don't want to know about it. Keep it to yourself.

2. Effective immediately, all one-on-one discussions outside of our rubber stamped, all rated the same, totally useless annual review will stop. There will be no further one-on-one discussions of our expectations, your progress, the company culture or the company vision.

You can figure this out on your own. We will no longer solicit your ideas for improvement, offer suggestions on how to improve your performance, make your job easier or give you praise. We realize this has not taken place in years, and we wanted to squelch the rumor we might begin informing, including or engaging you in the future.

We have no plans to introduce this time consuming, make you feel included process back into our culture. (Oh, wait, we don't have a culture. In fact, effective immediately, our culture is to not have a company culture. Tolerance of future behavior will establish our culture.) There have been reports of a few rouge leaders attempting to establish a culture, but it will cease immediately. We will not have isolated groups feeling informed, included and engaged.

3. Effective immediately, there will be no documented performance improvement plans or levels of discipline initiated on poor performers on quality, productivity, safety or attendance. Those of you that are high performers will have to pick up the slack. Since no one has ever been placed on a written performance improvement plan, a level of discipline or dismissed for poor performance in years, this will not be much of a change.

We can strive to improve in other ways, and we will let you know when these ways are discovered. We realize removing this paper trail virtually eliminates our ability to dismiss an employee for poor performance. Our response to this is "oh, well, we weren't doing it anyway. We just wouldn't formally admit it". We are now admitting it. No secrets. Full disclosure will be part of our new culture if we ever establish one!

This document serves as formal notice to all newly promoted leaders as we gradually remove all their pee and vinegar. We will gradually transition you into bosses that realize spending time on documentation is unnecessary and will not be tolerated.

Time spent documenting, addressing performance problems and developing team members is better spent on putting out fires and handling the same problems that occur day in and day out. Dismissals will only occur as a result of extreme misconduct or violating these rules. The practice of using documentation and the time-tested basic tools of leadership to improve performance have been discontinued effective today.

Note: All of "Our employees are our greatest asset" posters will remain on the wall. Our new mission statement will join each poster. "We know how we got here, and we believe with very little effort, we can stay here."

Signed, Your upper-level boss/employee mindsets

Does it hit close to home? You would NEVER say or write these words, but many of you may be in an environment where all three of these rules occur every single day. There is absolutely no documentation of education, engagement or accountability in your organization. This occurs from a lack of training and/or lack of accountability.

THIS is the reason 50-80% of employees are not satisfied in their positions. It has very little to do with the functions they perform. They signed on to perform the functions. It's the treatment and lack of inclusion they didn't expect.

(Note: If you are one of the bosses that say "they get their inclusion every other Friday OR if they don't like it, they are hiring at McDonalds", the very best thing you can do for your organization is resign.)

Whenever there is time or money spent, there are expectations. With every paycheck, there should be expectations. The consequences of not meeting those expectations should be performance improvement plans, discipline and ultimately dismissal. With every hour spent by a team member, there are expectations also. It should be fair treatment, a feeling of worth to the company and fair compensation.

When the expectations of the team member and the company are both met; your competition does not stand a chance.

Chapter 4. The Success Formula Of Education, Engagement and Accountability.

Successful, growing organizations are built around the three-legged stool of Education, Engagement and Accountability. You cannot shorten or eliminate any leg.

The best example I can give is early in my career as a new telephone installer repairman. They didn't just hand me a set of pole climbers or hooks as they were called and tell me to go climb a pole.

They didn't just hand me an installation order or repair ticket and tell me to go install or repair. I attended classes in installation, repair and pole climbing. This was my Education.

After completing my Education, I was given a set of reasonable expectations for quality, quantity, safety and attendance. My progress was reviewed on a monthly basis.

Even though I was one of three technicians in Ashdown, Arkansas and one of tens of thousands across the country, I knew what role I played in the success of my crew, District and company. This was my Engagement. This is the step that made me proud of what I did. This is the step that established my morale.

I was held accountable to consistently meet all expectations. Failure to do so would result in performance improvement plans or levels of discipline. A continued failure to meet expectations would result in termination. This was the Accountability portion of the success formula.

Fortunately, I always performed at a level to never experience this leg of the stool but I saw it used with poor performers. I knew without a doubt, Accountability was present, consistent and did not show favorites.

I always felt I was a good technician. It is simple when you are only responsible for your results and are using your hands.

When promoted to a supervisor, everything changed. It became more difficult and different. I had to produce the same quality, quantity, safety and attendance results through the hands of others.

I had to trade in my hooks and tool belt for a different set of tools. This toolbox contained the various tools of Education, Engagement and Accountability.

Let's take a closer look at Education, Engagement and Accountability.

Most organizations do not skip the Education step; especially in non-management. This is normally where the work gets done. These team members produce the product or provide the service. Organizations either Educate or hire someone with existing skills.

Education is sometimes forgotten when there are internal promotions. Many new managers and supervisors are expected to "go forth and lead". Leadership is like pole climbing. If experience is your only teacher; it will be a very costly, time-consuming and painful process.

The lack of Engagement is a huge problem. This problem has increased with the use of technology. Nothing will ever replace a one-on-one, face-to-face session. I have surveyed hundreds of managers with this question; "Not counting an annual review, when was the last time your immediate supervisor sat down with you one-on-one and reviewed expectations, your progress and your contribution to the organization?" My current statistic is 65% say Never. My favorite answer has been; "I can't remember the last time this occurred, but I know my hair was a different color."

The lack or absence of communication and Engagement are your greatest contributor to morale problems. It is also a major contributor to poor results, customer service and turnover.

I have worked with organizations where there is no accountability. It has been years since a team member has been placed on a performance improvement plan or level of discipline. My two questions to them are; "how are you improving" and "do your results reflect that you are so good that no one needs improvement?"

If every employee meets their expectations every year, your expectations are too low.

A few years ago I got my foot in the door with a 4000 person organization with this question; "How many team members are currently on a Performance Improvement Plan or level of discipline in your entire organization?" The answer was zero. When I asked what other leadership tools were being using to improve performance or change behavior, I received "a deer in the headlights look".

I gave the example of clicking two glasses together every New Years Eve as 4000 totally unaccountable years pass by.

I have been unable to find a better formula for personal or business success than Education, Engagement and Accountability. It is impossible to "get better" without all three. They work as a three part team, or they don't work at all.

I have also found it is impossible to increase Education, Engagement and Accountability and not get better in results, profitability, turnover and morale in ANY organization.

Chapter 5. Bring Back The Tight Ship!

There is a cliché I seldom hear anymore. It is acceptable if the cliché is outdated, but the concept should never go out of style. The cliché is; "they run a tight ship." This is an old nautical statement that was a compliment to the captain of a ship.

The captain is responsible for everything on the ship. He took personal responsibility. There was no finger pointing or "it's not my job".

The same should exist in every leadership position. Do you run a tight ship? Are you consistent in addressing poor performers? Are you consistent in praising your high performers?

The only way to run a tight ship is to plug your leaks. Poor performers, inconsistencies, poor customer service, high turnover, low morale and inefficiencies are your leaks. You will never get better and run a tight ship until these leaks are plugged. "They ran a tight ship" should be a statement we want associated with our legacy.

Chapter 6. The Benefit Of "Leading Like You Own It!"

I had shared my leadership and life lessons with hundreds of companies and thousands of attendees, but this company was different.

This company was doing something right. They had grown several times their original size in 12 years. They had requested my leadership seminar to be delivered one-on-one with every manager and non-management team member.

At the end of each session, I knew there was something special and unique going on. Every night I would tell my wife, Sandy, I didn't want this assignment to end. I was shifting from teacher to student many times during each session.

Every manager and non-management team member had a great attitude and acted as if they owned a part of the business, but they didn't. I checked. They were all salaried or hourly.

On the last day, I shared my seminar with the owner. This was conducted one-on-one, and there was plenty of time for interaction.

At the end of my session with the owner, he leaned back in his chair and said I helped him realize why he was doing what he was doing.

I asked if he would mind sharing his thoughts with me? He said, "my family have a lot going on in their lives. (Notice he said my family; not team members, employees or heaven forbid, subordinates.) They have health issues, money issues, relationship issues, marital problems, kid problems and have recently lost loved ones.

My job is to make sure this business is successful and profitable. My job is to make this company so solid that no family member that meets expectations has to worry about being laid off, part timed or having their pay or benefits cut."

I still get goose bumps when telling that story. He cared. This is what American business should be. You don't hear CNN or FOX talking about this when they talk about free enterprise.

My version of what he said was in a life full of variables, he wanted his company to be a constant in the lives of "his family."

I saw where the great attitudes and success of the company originated, but I still couldn't quite summarize the success of this company.

A week later at 4:00 AM, it hit me. I remember sitting straight up in bed. After hundreds of keynotes and leadership seminars with thousands of attendees; this was the first time; the only time; an owner had hired me.

Every other time, I've been hired by someone in an organizational chart or hierarchy.

Let me stop here to ask a question. Have you ever rented a car? Have you ever waxed it? Changed oil in it? Rotated the tires? I rent cars many times in business, and I must admit I've never had the urge to do any of these.

Why? We don't do these things because we don't own it. We have it for a short term. We don't abuse the car, but we certainly don't treat it like we own it. How many of us have treated different aspects of our life; our health, our finances, our relationships, our job or our career like a rental car? I do believe we can all raise our hands.

Working with this company is where the Leader/Owner mindset originated. Every team member of every company will have one of three mindsets; Leader/Owner, boss/employee or employee. The Leader/Owner is not restricted to management, and the employee only mindset is not restricted to non-management.

Their performance and attitude will match their mindset. If they feel no sense of ownership and pride, it will be reflected in their performance and attitude.

This mindset begins with the leadership of an organization. Evidently, this owner was doing something right to experience this level of growth. His Leader/Owner mindset permeated throughout the entire organization.

He made long-term decisions. He probably wouldn't wax a rental car either but when it came to his business, he owned it and expected each "family member" to also treat it like they owned it.

When we make decisions that have better long-term results, it seems everything works better.

"If you can lead one, you can lead many. If you can't lead one, you can't lead any." - Unknown

Let's get to some lessons that allow you to appreciate The Power Of Better!

Chapter 7. Have Any Great Supervisors, Managers or Leaders Been Born In Your Company?

I recently read a story by John Maxwell about leaders being born in a quaint European village. I want to put my own spin on the story but I give John the credit for this example and inspiration.

I'm from Hope, Arkansas, and as you know, there are a couple of well-known politicians born in Hope. I've spoken all over the country, and I am constantly asked if I know Mike or Bill. Luckily there is one from each political party so I don't feel uncomfortable sharing this story. Also, this story is about leadership; not politics.

A group of European tourists were touring Hope, Arkansas, a small town in the southwest corner of the state. They visited the Watermelon Festival, Clinton's birthplace, the downtown area, some of the local businesses and a few of the churches. A few of the European tourists were very excited about the history of this small town.

While dining at one of the local restaurants, one of the tourist engaged an elderly man in conversation about the town. He discovered the elderly gentleman had lived there his entire life. Eager to hear more about the town's history he asked the elderly gentleman "Have any great men, women or leaders been born here?" "Nope," said the elderly gentlemen, "only babies."

I thought this was a great example of the value of what we are exposed to in our life. I do not believe people are born as a great leader, supervisor or manager, anymore than a person is born a great brain surgeon. I truly believe it is what we read, listen to, watch, attend and the people we are around that shape us into something different than what we are. This can be good or bad. All true leaders were born "a baby".

Have any great leaders, managers or supervisors been "born" in your company? Did they bring their skill sets with them? Did you provide the training or was that brutal, expensive, time-consuming teacher called experience the one responsible for most of the changes in your organization?

Chapter 8. Your Very Own Widget Factory.

To get you in the proper frame of mind to Lead Like You Own It and see the Power Of Better, I want you to own your very own Widget Factory.

Your rich uncle just passed away and left you a Widget Factory. These are the numbers.

- You have ten team members that make an average of eight widgets a day each, and you pay them $10 an hour.
- There is a supervisor at the factory that makes $45,000 a year.
- The widgets sell for $10 each and the factory sells all they make at a store on the property. The person in the store also makes $10 an hour.
- Your daily revenue is $800, and you pay $800 a day in wages, not counting the supervisor and the store keeper.

It is obvious your rich uncle was subsidizing this operation. He did not leave you any of his money. Are you happy? What are you going to do? You can't sell it because no one wants a Widget Factory headed for disaster.

Hints: There are no hints! YOU are the owner. You figure it out. This is what leaders do. They solve problems. Don't read any farther until you develop ideas on your own.

There are two main items you would look at with a Leader/Owner Mindset. One of these is to examine your productivity. Why are you only averaging eight widgets a day? Do you have some averaging four and others averaging 12? See if there are training or systems that can increase your productivity. Just imagine what increasing your productivity to 12-14 widgets per person per day would do to your profitability.

The other item I would look at would be the price of the widget. Since you are selling all you produce; who says the market wouldn't pay more? Increase the price of your widgets. See what the market will pay. What if you could receive $12-$15 per widget? That would make a huge difference in your profitability.

If you can make enough improvements in one or both of these items to make your organization profitable and sustainable, you may consider adding to your workforce. You could even consider broadening your market. I don't know what a widget weighs or what it costs to ship a widget, but you could consider the WWWW, the World Wide Widget Web. The World Wide Widget Web should ONLY be considered when you are profitable.

Did you feel The Power Of Better? How did it feel to turn an organization around that was certainly destined for layoffs and closure? How did it feel to save and protect the livelihoods of others like yourself? After it turned around, how did it feel to add positions and provide a livelihood for other families? That is truly a benefit of "getting better". That's what Leader-Owners do.

Chapter 9. The RIPM. (Retired In Place Manager)

The worst part of the Human Resources assignment is being involved in terminations. Over my career, I was involved in many terminations, and the last one was no easier than the first. Even though each ex-employee chose termination through their performance or behavior, it never became easier.

As a result of their productivity and attendance, we terminated a 20+ year employee. This individual and I lived in the same town. I had not seen him for two years since he left the employment of the company. One day in a local store, we each rounded the end of an aisle at the same time and met face-to-face.

He said, "Greg Gilbert, I've been thinking about you." My first thought was if there was a firearm or explosive device nearby. He stuck out his hand, smiled and said I've meant to call you. He said I want to thank you for your involvement in my dismissal. Now friends, if I had a nickel for every time I've heard that, I would have a nickel.

He said it was not your fault or my bosses fault I lost my job. It was my fault. I had a drinking problem. I let it get the best of me. He also said I know what you did for me, and I do appreciate it. You see, our company policy allowed for dismissed employees to receive full benefits and access to our Employee Assistance Program for the remainder of the calendar month after dismissal.

I wasn't certain, but I suspected substance abuse, so I left this individual on suspension until the first day of the month. I made the dismissal effective on the first. Unknown to me, he had taken advantage of our employee assistance program during that month.

He said he had a new job; it wasn't as good as his previous job, but everything was going his way. He also said he had not drank in over two years since his dismissal. He said his life was better and he appreciated my involvement. We had a good 20-minute visit. We shook hands and parted ways. When I got in my truck, I got angry again. Here's why.

You see, Ten months prior to this individual losing their job, his boss retired. Excuse me, let me clarify. His boss made it official. His boss had been retired in place for quite some time. We have all heard of RIP (Rest In Peace), well, he was RIP (Retired In Place). When his boss retired or made it official, a new manager took responsibility for the crew.

The new manager did what a manager is expected and paid to do. He looked at which crew members were not carrying their load. This individual stuck out like a sore thumb. The new manager placed the individual on performance improvement plans and different levels of discipline, but the performance and behavior did not improve. Ten months after the new manager took over, this 22-year employee was terminated due to poor performance and attendance.

Here's what made me angry. As I prepared the separation proposal, I saw the trend begin two years prior to the retirement of his boss. I saw a 20+ year employee with perfect attendance began missing Mondays and Fridays. Would you like to take a guess what his boss did about this? You are right. Nothing!

On paper, I also saw a 20+ year employee consistently in the top two performers in his crew, drop to the bottom. Would you like to take a guess what his boss did about this? You are right. Nothing! I saw a 20+ year employee with zero accidents have two motor vehicle accidents in three weeks. You know the routine now. The boss did nothing about this.

I am in HR person at heart, and I like to deal with facts. I don't like to play "what if" games. But I cannot get it out of my heart if we had begun with an EAP Referral, performance improvement plans and levels of discipline immediately when the problem began; we might have salvaged a great long term team member.

Even though I do not take any of the responsibility away from the person with the drinking problem, we failed as the leadership team.

This is a story of a person with a leader owner mindset and a person with a boss-employee mindset. The manager with a leader-owner mindset did what he was paid to do and led like he owned it. The boss-employee mindset ignored the problem and his job responsibilities.

You may have the same question I have. How did the boss-employee mindset stick around long enough to retire? This occurs in every organization across the country. It is a lack of accountability.

If you are not willing to hold poor performers accountable or are unwilling to use the leadership tools available, do your team members and company a favor. Get out. That's right. Get out. You do not deserve to be in leadership and you are putting the livelihoods of others in jeopardy. If it because of a lack of training, seek training. If it is a lack of guts or want to, get out.

Chapter 10. You Have A Team, Be A Coach!

The English term "coach" is derived from a medium of transport that traces its origins to the Hungarian word kocsi meaning "carriage" that was named after the village where it was first made.

The first use of the term coaching to mean an instructor or trainer arose around 1830 at Oxford University. It was slang for a tutor who "carries" a student through an exam. Coaching thus has been used in language to describe the process used to transport people from where they are, to where they want to be. The first use of the term in relation to sports came in 1861.

Can you see the value of acting as a coach even though your title may be manager or supervisor? Isn't it your main goal to get each team member from where they are to where they need to be? That's what a stage coach, flying coach and a motor coach accomplishes. Why not you?

Chapter 11. The Greatest Bang For Your Time.

If you owned a widget factory and there was a high demand for widgets, would you rather have ten team members or one producing widgets? That's an easy question. Ten can easily out produce one.

If you are a manager or supervisor, I would like for you to think about the greatest bang for your time, not your money. When I was promoted, I went from a telephone technician to a supervisor of a crew with ten telephone technicians. I had to achieve the same results I produced with my hands in the past through the hands of others.

I was not paid to install or repair phones as a supervisor. I had ten very capable technicians that were paid and expected to take care of those tasks. As a supervisor, I was held accountable for quality, quantity, safety and attendance. These were the same expectations of the technicians.

How much actual time do we spend as a supervisor growing, developing and helping our team get better? My guess is this is a minimal amount of time. If you are unsure, track it. Most of us have smart phones with a timer. Pick a week. Track the amount of time spent developing team members. The majority of your 40-60-hour week will be busy putting out fires, handling problems and other busy work. Activity does not equal productivity.

There is a gold mine of better results, customer service and morale right below the surface. It requires no digging, just a few hours per week spent developing your team. A small percentage of improvement multiplied by the number of team members will go a long way in protecting livelihoods. That is a great reason to get better and a tremendous bang for your time.

Chapter 12. Put Me On Discipline. Please!

The similarities in the three stories were spooky. I had just shared my program with three different companies in three different locations in three weeks. At the end of each of these three programs, an individual shared a personal story with me. The stories were nearly identical with different players, but the message was the same.

I will share one of the stories. Keep in mind, these were all three managers that shared their stories.

"Mr. Gilbert, I can truly relate to what you said about the need for Accountability. Years ago, I wasn't a very good employee. I had a problem with punctuality and absence. My manager met with me and covered the future consequences of this continued low performance. I continued to miss days. I was suspended for one day.

This suspension did not equate to much money, so it had no impact. I remember going to the lake and having fun. When I returned to work, my manager told me future occurrences would lead to higher levels of discipline up to and including dismissal.

A few weeks later, I was late again. I was immediately suspended for three days without pay. This hurt. I didn't go to the lake. I stayed home and realized I was probably on the verge of losing my job. I was right. When I returned to work, I was informed future occurrences would lead to termination.

My entire commitment and attitude toward my job changed in those three days at home. I am so grateful for a manager that held me and everyone in our crew totally accountable. This change in attitude resulted in a total turnaround of my work ethic and performance. A few years later I was promoted. I hold my team totally accountable. I owe it all to _____ (all three said a name). They changed my life.

All three individuals were so appreciative of a manager that held them and others totally accountable. These three stories in three weeks amplified the importance of great leaders.

Each of these three individuals gave the credit for their turnaround and subsequent promotion to one leader. Could you be that leader? If not, what has to change to make you that leader? Maybe your plan to get better should include holding yourself and others more accountable. If this is not in your plan, get out of leadership. You are putting livelihoods in jeopardy.

Chapter 13. Never Assume! ALWAYS Clarify!

I must cover a leadership lesson involving a chicken house.

When I was 13 years old, I owned my own hay hauling and basic farm labor business. I thought I was leading like I owned it. One week, I made a mistake. This mistake allowed me to participate in that old cliché, "experience is the best teacher.

One of my hay hauling customers had a chicken house. He asked if I would clean out his chicken house. I agreed because all I saw was income opportunity for the business.

In those days, there were no tractors or front end loaders involved. It was done with a large scoop, a wheel barrow, hundreds of trips and plenty of sweat equity. Before you get the wrong impression, this was not his chicken house for a few laying hens. This was a chicken house for thousands of chickens and measured approximately 24 X 60 feet.

I don't remember the time involved, but I do remember it being many days of work. It was thousands of scoops of chicken manure, sawdust and hundreds of wheel barrow loads.

Upon completion, I drove my 53 Chevy, (I had bought this for $50 with hay hauling money and was restricted to dirt roads since I didn't have a license.) to the owners home for my compensation. He said he would ride with me back to the chicken house for a quality inspection prior to payment. I had no problem with this because I had the concrete floor clean enough for an old-fashioned barn dance.

We arrived at the chicken house, and he proceeded to check the results of my work. He was satisfied and I remember him making what I call a BPM, (Back Pocket Move). He pulled out a leather wallet that appeared to be from a Tandy Leather Wallet Kit. He tilted the wallet back towards himself so I was unable to see the contents. In anticipation, I watched his thumb and pointing finger squeeze and rub each bill to insure there was no "double payment."

He first handed me a five. I thanked him knowing this would be the first of many visits to the wallet. The next trip only produced a one. I was okay knowing there would be many more visits to the wallet. He again pulled out a one. I thanked him, assuming there were many more wallet trips to follow. I was wrong. The wallet went back into his pocket. He stuck his hand out, thanked me and asked me if I could drive him back to his house.

I was so shocked, I shook his hand and agreed to drive him home before you could say "seven stinking dollars." I dropped him off, backed into the road and probably threw a little gravel as I headed home. After just being a victim of what I considered felony extortion, I barely heard him yell he would call me again when it needed cleaning.

I was hot! Seven dollars for cleaning out a chicken house? I needed some counsel and sympathy. Mom and Dad would be home in a few hours. I couldn't wait until they got home. I knew Dad would help me correct this huge injustice. I was wrong.

After I had told the story of the highway robbery, my anger increased as my Dad began laughing. I thought he would never quit. I failed to see the humor and began questioning his love for me. After my Dad finally quit laughing and using his hanky to wipe both eyes, he asked one question; what price did I agree on before I began?

I said I didn't quote him a price but...but...but. My Dad didn't want to hear the buts. I remember his words as if they were yesterday; "Son, you have just received a great life lesson, and you made $7.00 while you were learning. People pay money to learn these in college.

This is what happens when you allow another person to establish your value, and you don't know what value they placed on your work. This must be established up front when both parties have a chance to walk away from the established value. Consider it a lesson and move on."

It was obvious Dad wasn't planning on having a talk with the felon that had just robbed me of what I consider a full weeks pay... but he was right. When I hauled hay, I let the customer know up front what I charged. If they tried to negotiate, we both had the opportunity to walk away.

Although I would've taken the money at that age, I am so thankful my Dad didn't try to "make it better" by slipping me a twenty.

Thankfully, there was no "bailout program" for foolish 13-year-olds. That would have totally removed the lesson. If you are the parent that constantly bails out your kids, shame on you. You are treating them like a rental car and making short term decisions with long term negative impacts. Teach them to take ownership of their actions. There MUST be a consequence to change performance or behavior.

Every job I have held in my life has been an agreement for my work in exchange for their pay. I knew what they wanted, and I knew what they paid. If they hired me and I didn't fulfill the job requirements, they could walk away. If I thought the pay was too low for the value I bring to the job, I could walk away. We should agree on the price before we pick up the scoop and wheel barrow.
I was NOT leading like I owned it. I displayed no leadership or responsibility when I agreed to the chicken house job. Luckily, no family members or team members were placed in jeopardy because of my inexperience and ignorance.

What value do you bring to your job or career? Want more money? Bring more value. Take ownership.

Chapter 14. Your Influence Goes Deeper Than An Org Chart

In 2012, I was privileged to have the opportunity to speak to a group of managers for Red River Army Depot in Texarkana, Texas. I was probably 30 minutes into my presentation when I had what we call in the speaking industry, a brain fart. I totally lost where I was in my presentation due to a thought crossing my mind.

You see there is an old cliché that says we should learn, earn and return. Both of my parents had retired with over 30 years of service at Red River Army Depot. It hit me I was giving back to an organization that fed, clothed and put a roof over my head as a child. I recovered quickly and probably no one noticed the delay but me.

After my presentation, I contacted both of my grown daughters to ask them a question. The question was; did you ever hear me whine, moan and complain about my job, career or a manager while I was at Southwestern Bell? Both daughters gave the same answer; no dad, you loved it.

This took me back to growing up on the farm. I spent hundreds of hours working on equipment with my dad in an old barn. He talked a lot about his job, but I cannot ever remember him whining, moaning or complaining about his job, a manager or the Commanding Officer. The same was true of my mom. They both enjoyed their job and appreciated the opportunities provided by Red River Army Depot.

It made me realize my mom and dad's leaders were not only leading Thomas and Virginia Gilbert, they were also leading a kid named Greg Gilbert. When I went to work for Southwestern Bell, I went looking for what was right. I didn't go looking for what was wrong. Looking back, I attribute this totally to my parents and their leaders.

I guess you can say they led like they owned it. Keep this in mind as you lead, guide and influence others in your life and career. Your impact goes much deeper than an organizational chart.

Chapter 15. They Don't Pay Me What I'm Worth

Speaking of what value we bring to the job reminds me of a friend that at least twice a week, would say these words; they don't pay me what I'm worth.

After years of hearing this, I finally grew tired of his comment and finally prepared my response. I knew I wouldn't have to wait long.

That week during a conversation, he finally said it again; you know Greg, they just don't pay me what I'm worth. I shocked him. I agreed with him and said; "you are very lucky there is a minimum wage law that prevents the company from paying you what you are worth." It went right over his head, and he agreed with me.

An hour didn't pass until my phone rang with him asking for an apology. He just realized what I had said. I apologized and told him I knew he gave the company 100% every week. He gave them 20% on Monday, 20% on Tuesday, etc. We had a good laugh, but I didn't hear the "they don't pay me what I'm worth" comment ever again.

Do they pay you what you are worth? If not; whose fault is it? Who is in error? Is it the fault of your company or you?

What is the basis for this mindset? If it is truly based on market value, you should have no trouble in turning in your resignation and finding someone that will "pay you what you are worth."

Is it based on the fact you don't enjoy your job and you feel you should be paid more to do something you don't enjoy? If you don't enjoy your job, it will be reflected in your results and attitude.

I have never been forced at gunpoint to accept a job. Every position I have held was a result of me making a verbal request or filling out an application. I requested to work there.

Once you have the mindset they are not paying what you are worth, I truly believe most will begin subconsciously adjusting their contribution to a lower level. This creates a mediocre team and ultimately puts pay, benefits and livelihoods in jeopardy. If you have this mindset; do you and your team members a favor; change the mindset or quit and look elsewhere.

The Leader/Owner Mindset looks for ways to add value to their organization. The boss/employee or the employee mindsets are more likely to have a "they don't pay me what I'm worth" and "where is the greener grass" mindset.

What are you doing to insure you are compensated for the value you bring? When you feel there is a fair exchange of value between you, your employer and your customer; that's when you are leading like you own it. That's when you "get better".

Chapter 16. Seniority Vs. Results - Who Wins?

Circle your answers below:

Seniority should be <u>Rewarded</u> and/or <u>Celebrated</u>. (Circle all that apply.)

Results should be <u>Rewarded</u> and/or <u>Celebrated</u>. (Circle all that apply.)

You may have your own thoughts on this but after years of management and Human Resources in a union environment, here are my thoughts;

Seniority should be Celebrated.

Results should be Rewarded AND Celebrated.

Seniority may be considered a display of loyalty but Results keep your doors open. Let me give you another example where you may be able to gain a little more clarity on this situation;

You and your family are attending a football game with your favorite college team. The conference championship will be determined by who wins this game. With tickets, parking, matching jerseys and refreshments; you are more than a just a fan. You are fully invested and engaged in this game.

The game goes back and forth. It is very exciting. The game comes down to the final two seconds. Your team is two points behind. Your team is on their twenty-yard line and can win it with a field goal. Your team has two field goal kickers. One is a senior and it is his final game. He hasn't kicked since the beginning of the season. The other is a sophomore, more accurate and has made 100% of his attempts from within the 30-yard line.

Who do you want kicking the ball? Results or Seniority? Are you leaning towards letting the senior have a chance since it's his last game? I'm betting not. Wins keep butts in the seats and donations coming to the scholarship program. Wins are results. Seniority is just, well, Seniority.

In your Widget Factory example, which would you rather have in your organization; Results or Seniority?

Last year I heard my absolute favorite comeback concerning seniority. I was working with an organization that for years had promoted on the sole attribute of seniority. A few years ago they realized the train wreck created by this practice.

They changed the practice to begin considering performance, contribution, attitude and ability to work with others. This, as in any change of long term practices or culture, creates happiness in the ones who benefit from the change and will anger the ones that feel slighted.

This attendee came up to me after a program. She had been promoted a few months earlier and had eight years with the organization. Another person in her organization with 20 years of service felt she should have received the promotion. She let the newly promoted manager know it on a regular basis. Finally after months of constant harassment, the newly promoted manager stated a fact that stopped the comments.

The 20-year team member told the newly promoted manager one more time; "I should have gotten that promotion. I've been here 20 years." The newly promoted manager responded with "That filing cabinet has been here 20 years also, but that means absolutely NOTHING. I'm tired of hearing about it." The comments stopped.

What a great example. The filing cabinet did everything it was asked to do over the last 20 years, but it did absolutely nothing extra. Are you doing only what you are asked? If you lead like you own it, you are always looking for ways to improve yourself, your position and the organization.

Chapter 17. Honesty And Integrity - The Most Valuable Leadership Trait

I was recently contacted by a friend and asked what I considered the most important leadership quality. I didn't have to blink or think. It was honesty and integrity. Skills can be taught, but honesty and integrity can make or break companies, organizations and families.

In 1989 when I arrived in my human resources position, one of my mentors and predecessors, Jim McMains, shared these exact words with me;

"Greg, you can work on an employee's quality, quantity, safety and attendance, but you cannot instill honesty and integrity in a person. They either have it, or they don't. You will never be good enough nor lucky enough to catch a thief the first time he steals from you, and until he changes his heart, he will steal from you again."

I found these words to be so true; especially in cases of second chances.

A few years ago I had lunch with a friend. As we parted ways, he stated, well, you are more honest on that than I would be. About 30 minutes later it hit me. You can't put the word more in front of honest. We are either honest or we're not. You can put an ER on the end of fast, smart, quick or slow but we cannot be honestER.

I learned years ago reputations are very important. In fact, reputations come in a very limited supply. I look at everything I do and say as building my reputation. I look at everything I do and say as building my reputation like a wall, one brick at a time.

Whenever I do or say something that hurts my reputation, I'm not allowed to take a brick from the top of the wall. I have to dig down and take a brick from the foundation. As you can imagine, it won't take the removal of many bricks from the foundation before my reputation begins to crumble.

You can rebuild a reputation but why not just prevent the ruin of your reputation? Continue to build a good reputation one-word and action at a time.

Chapter 18. You Are The Difference

A company can change computers, change software, upgrade machinery, change systems, change management, even change ownership, but as long as you have the ability to get a group of people to work with you, to go in a common direction, develop people, produce and improve results with integrity, you greatly increase your value to an organization. There will always be a demand for these abilities. You would not believe the phenomenal changes you can make in your organization by just becoming "brilliant in the basics".

All organizations have access to the same processes, software, machinery and raw materials. The only things that will differentiate your organization from your competition are you and the members of your team.

Too many people do their work in a mediocre way and hope inertia will carry them through a day, week, year or even a career. I know you've heard of RIP, Rest in Peace, some team members are Retired In Place.

They have the idea when the right job comes along, then they will really work hard. But the right job never comes along. They are always passed over for promotions. They are always the last ones hired, the first ones laid off and the one pointing the finger at the company and blaming others instead of looking in the mirror.

Every one of us is where we are in life because of the best decisions we've made so far. How's that working for us?

Chapter 19. The Leadership Tool Kit

Every successful leader has a "Leadership Tool Kit". The tools inside consist of:

- communication skills,
- honesty and integrity,
- performance improvement plans
- different levels of discipline
- terminations
- compassion
- trust
- the desire to hold themselves and others accountable
- the ability to delegate tasks AND outcomes
- a vision for the company and team members
- humility
- character
- compassion.

Did you notice there is no hammer in this tool kit? Did you notice I listed compassion twice?

Did you also notice there is no intimidation, demeaning others, degrading others, talking to team members about other team members, yelling or screaming in the Leadership Tool Kit? If you have any of these in your leadership toolkit you have two choices; remove them or remove yourself from leadership. Livelihoods are at stake.

Yelling and screaming are the greatest short-term, rental car examples I can give. They may work short-term but will lead to excessive turnover and morale problems in the future.

Every one of us can think of bosses that use yelling, screaming, demeaning others and intimidation as their preferred leadership style. This style of management was never effective long term and should have died with disco music in the late 1970's.

Do whatever it takes to stock your toolkit with the good items, eliminate the bad items. Educate or eliminate those that still use yelling and screaming as leadership tools. (See the chapter on the line in the sand.)

Chapter 20. Two High And Two Low

For this chapter, let's pretend you are my HR Manager. I am a first level field supervisor. You have requested we meet for lunch. I have been struggling with my results. My turnover has also been increasing.

I have ten technicians on my team. After ordering our food, you ask this question;

"Imagine you had to go from ten technicians to eight technicians. Do you know the two technicians you could lose and hurt the least? Since this is hypothetical, I immediately say yes, I know the two that would hurt me the least.

You then ask if I had to downsize from ten technicians to two, did I know the two I would keep. Again, since this is hypothetical, I immediately say yes, I know the two I would keep.

You then ask the tough question; can you tell the difference between the two you would keep and the two you would lose on paper? What are you doing to raise the level of performance on the two you would lose?

Now, let's reverse roles. I'm the HR Manager. How would you answer these questions? If you are doing nothing, how is your team getting better?

This is a great exercise to make us think. I always did this one-on-one. Never in public. It brings a lack of improvement to the manager's attention.

Chapter 21. I Would Have Done A Better Job If I'd Known We Were Going To Lay People Off!

Let's dive deeper to see the greater impact of leaders shunning their responsibilities.

Downsizing, layoffs, force massaging, trimming the rose bush, interruption in work status, reorganization, restructuring. It doesn't matter what you call it; it is painful. It impacts employees and families. In many cases, I believe "due to the economy" is used frequently because it sounds so much better than "due to crappy leadership".

We were very fortunate to go without layoffs for many years. Then it changed. Because we had a labor agreement, non-management was laid off by seniority. Management downsized by a combination of seniority and annual reviews.

I had the unpleasant task of administering a management downsizing in the 90's. I labeled it Octoberfest. It was painful watching good people in jeopardy or what I came to call "below the line" and not so good managers remain "above the line". Many were "above the line" due to seniority and a weak appraisal system.

Don't get me wrong, I'm not against seniority if everything is equal but in most cases, nothing is equal. If leaders consistently do what they are paid to do and weed out poor performers, you wouldn't see good team members leave and poor performers stay. In fact, consistently getting better and doing what we are paid to do as a leader would probably prevent the need for a layoff.

Let's look at the impact of a RIPM (Retired In Place Manager) that ignores poor performers, loads his high performers up and rubber stamps all appraisals to look the same. I've seen this occur. His junior crew members are carrying most of the load. His senior crew members believe they have asbestos underwear (fireproof) and do just enough to get by.

For whatever reason, there is a downsizing and the manager must lose three team members. Because everyone looks the same on paper and there is no performance improvement plans or levels of discipline, he loses the three junior team members.

When you look closely, these three team members were 30% of the crew but were doing 60% of the work.

Low tide has just arrived and this Retired In Place Manager has been caught skinny dipping. How could this have been prevented? By constantly getting better. You get better by working with your poor performers.

Are you making your numbers? Do you even have numbers? In this business environment, we better all have our numbers and use every leadership tool available to make our numbers.

Chapter 22. Attendance - I Need You At Work And On Time. Enough Said!

The latest figures I've read stated absence costs American businesses 8.7% of their annual payroll. That is a huge expense that in many cases, goes ignored. I've seen a trend since FMLA was passed, to ignore absence. There are plenty of non-FMLA absences that need to be addressed.

When FMLA was passed, my absence increased by 40% over the next year, so it made it even MORE important to address non-FMLA absences. I believe FMLA is really an acronym for Find My Lost Attendance.

I love addressing attendance because it is not subjective. Either your rear is in a chair or it is not. I also do not get caught up in whether you were really sick or not. I give you that. (See B. below) I knew you would either maintain good attendance or eventually be seeking employment elsewhere.

Good attendance should be a condition of continued employment. That's a strong statement. Let me repeat. Good attendance should be a condition of continued employment. I want to share some guidelines taken from different companies and some of my ideas. You may already have attendance guidelines. This is not intended to change your current procedures unless your current procedures involve doing nothing.

Number One, company XYZ. To provide dependable service to our customers and remain a profitable enterprise, we must rely on our employees to be on the job. Each employee, management and non-management as a condition of employment, accepts the responsibility of being on the job as scheduled.

Number Two, company ABC. Our company policy on absence is good attendance and punctuality are required. While it is recognized an occasional absence is sometimes unavoidable, the company expects its employees to maintain reasonable health standards, take intelligent precautions against illness and accidents and not allow minor inconveniences to keep them away from the job. Good attendance means a demonstrated ability to be on the job, on time, over sustained periods of time.

Number Three, company DEF. Management is responsible for managing the attendance of each assigned employee. It is each manager's responsibility to explain to those employees under his or her supervision what is expected concerning attendance. There is no absolute numerical standard for determining good or bad attendance.

The determination of whether a particular employee's attendance is satisfactory or not will be made on an individual basis taking into account all the relevant factors pertaining to each employee's attendance record. Some of the common factors taken into account in evaluating each case are:

A. The number and frequency of absence and tardiness.
B. The reason for the absence and tardiness.
C. The employee's history of absence and tardiness.
D. The amount of time lost.
E. The employee's attitude toward maintaining satisfactory attendance.
F. The prognosis of the employee's attendance for the future.
G. Whether the absence qualifies under the Family And Medical Leave Act.

No disciple should be administered for absences covered under FMLA.

Most companies have a benefits plan or a compensation plan that allows for pay of x number of sick days per year. That includes both incidental absences and disability absences. This plan is in place to cover the compensation for absences. It does not set the standard for job performance. A paid sick day means you will suffer no loss in pay. It does NOT mean you will suffer no consequences as a result of paid absences.

Compensation and attendance accountability are totally different issues and are confused by many. Before you get into the compensation versus attendance discussion, be sure and check with your human resources department.

This is as simple as I can make absence. EVERY manager and supervisor should have a reasonable objective for non-FMLA absence. If they are not meeting that objective, they should be able to produce documentation of the performance improvement plans and levels of discipline being utilized to address absence and "get better". To not address non-FMLA absence is ignoring a huge waste of company time and money.

While the boss-employee mindset is saying "but they were really sick," the Leader-Owner Mindset is addressing the absence.

Chapter 23. Are You For Me Or Against Me?

Are you;

- For Me?
- Against Me?
- For Yourself?

What a great question. I recently surveyed a large organization with that question. I asked 150 managers to answer that question about their immediate supervisor. They were requested to answer anonymously on a 3 x 5 index card. Seventy percent of the managers responded their immediate supervisor was either against them or for themselves.

Are you surprised they had a huge morale and turnover problem? Of course not. I have been very fortunate in my career that every leader I have worked with has been for me. As a result of that support; I would walk through walls for each one of those leaders.

If you have team members that believe you are against them or for yourself, one of two things will occur;

1. They will do just enough to get by.
2. They will leave.

The only exception to this rule is the 3% to 5% that don't need leadership. They will do a phenomenal job on their own. The problem is, you cannot build a successful organization with this 3 to 5%. They will eventually grow tired of your incompetence and leave.

Oh, another thing to consider if you plan on leading AND living like you own it; this rule also applies outside the workplace. To have a successful marriage, family and friendships, the other parties must know you are for them, not against them or for yourself. I have seen some marriages where the spouses were not even in the same library much less on the same page.

Chapter 24. Trust, Guts And The Benefit Of Both!

I share my leadership seminar in different cities around the country. I share this in two different manners. The first is I am invited to present "The Power Of Better!" on-site at leadership meetings and conferences.

The second method is by picking a location and notifying local industry of the seminar. I normally pick the smaller locations because they normally have limited access to leadership development. In many cases, I will partner with a SHRM group, Chamber or local college.

During the notification of the local seminars, I receive many "we do our own training" answers. I understand this because I worked for an organization that "did our own training." The difference was we were always open to an outside perspective. Most of our "internal training" was designed to prepare team members to be able to successfully perform their job. We allowed external courses for additional growth and development.

Leadership development is not an exact science. Although I do believe in the success of "becoming brilliant in the basics," I don't believe in a cookie cutter approach. That is the beauty and challenge of dealing with people. We are all unique.

As the primary Human Resources contact of 2200 team members, I was never arrogant enough to believe we could not benefit from an outside perspective. Today, I am also not arrogant enough to believe "Leading Like You Own It!" is the cure all for every management problem.

In 2014, while calling industries to notify them of an upcoming seminar, I ran into this response; "I can't talk to you and you can't talk to me. I can't make any decisions. It all must go through corporate. They never ask for my two cents worth and there is absolutely no need to e-mail the information to me." When I tried to give her the website of the seminar, she wouldn't take it.

I finally got a laugh when I asked if she would give me her two cents worth if I offered a penny for her thoughts. Do you think she felt valued? Empowered? Do you think she felt her leadership was "For her", "Against her" or "For themselves?"
She was unwilling to even hear the website and review the free tools for managers. I felt as if I was attempting to hand her a Bible on a busy street in Communist China.

This reminded me of a situation early in my management career when I became aware of outside leadership development courses. I was looking for new tools for my leadership tool box. This occurred over 30 years ago. I will use my course as an example;

Note to my manager,

Bob,

There is a manager seminar coming to the area. It's titled "Leading Like You Own It!" It is two hours and the investment is $97. It's based on real-life successes, failures and what led to each in leadership and life.

It has great reviews and I would like to attend with your permission. The web site is www.LeadingLikeYouOwnIt.com

Let me know so I can register. Seating is limited.

Thank you,

Greg

I've sent a few notes like this to my leaders through the years until I received this note over 30 years ago.

Greg,

I received your request to attend the leadership seminar on xx-xx-xx. You have responsibility for producing results and a million dollar budget.

In the future, I trust your judgment. We both benefit from your leadership development. I don't scrutinize every $100 expenditure you make, and I'm not starting now. Remember rule # 1; If I have to do your job, I don't need you. Besides, if you pick up one idea to bring back, it's worth it.

FYI me on these in the future because I may also attend. I will let you know if I hear of any similar courses in the area.

Bob

Pay close attention to this leadership lesson.

When I received this note, do you think I believed my leadership was willing to invest in my success?

Do you believe I felt trusted?

Do you think I felt empowered?

Do you think I felt he was:

For Me?
Against me?
For himself?

When your team knows you are "For Them", they will walk through walls for you.

If they believe you are "Against Them" or "For Yourself", they will do just enough to get by OR leave UNLESS they are the less than 5% that will do the right thing even in the absence of leadership. You cannot build a successful team with only that 5% AND they will eventually leave incompetent leadership.

Even though my company had internal training, every leader I worked with was open to outside perspectives.

Do you think Bob had the guts to make this decision on HIS own? You bet he did. He had a multi-million dollar budget and was not being scrutinized on HIS $100 decisions.

Are you willing to forward an e-mail of a $100 leadership development seminar to your leadership team and allow them to decide whether to attend or not? You would find out who sees the value of personal development. That is Leading Like You Own It.

While we are on the subject of trust, let me share something I wrote in my journal years ago. *My high on trust, low on rules organization will always beat your high on rules low on trust organization.*

I had also written in my journal this statement; **Rules Minus A Relationship Equals Rebellion.** I'm not positive, but there were probably two teenage daughters at home when I wrote this in my journal.

Upon recently revisiting my journal, I realized this applies to all ages. I'm not referring to the type of rebellion that overthrows a company. I'm referring to the type of rebellion that does just enough to get by and cost companies billions of dollars every year.

Also, I would like to talk about guts for a minute. One of my HR partners and I were recently talking leadership. Roy said when he was promoted to management, his manager said these words; "Welcome to management. You now have more authority than you have guts to use." Roy kept talking as I tried to find pen and paper. I finally had to say, Roy, please stop talking for a minute. That is a very profound statement, and I must write that down. I have shared that statement with thousands.

I have changed that statement to read; When you are promoted into management, you have more authority and leadership tools than you have knowledge, confidence and guts to use. The goal of this book is to provide the leadership tools and the knowledge to improve your leadership ability. You will have to bring your own authority, confidence and guts to the party. When all of these come together, you will then lead like you own it. BYOG (Bring Your Own Guts)

Chapter 25. Whenever Money or Time Is Invested, There Are Expectations!

Expectations accompany expense. If you or I pay for something, there are expectations. If we incur an expense for a cheeseburger, shirt, car or house, we have expectations. A paycheck is an expense. There are expectations that accompany this expense.

The expectations of an employer must be written, clear and should be covered regularly. If the only time expectations and results are covered is an annual review, you have no expectations.

In fact, one of the best ways to measure the performance of your leadership team is to look at the number of written improvement plans or accolades in the past 60-90 days. If the number is between low and zero, no improvement or praise exists. You cannot afford to have leadership just report to work, distribute tasks, handle problems, go home and repeat tomorrow. They MUST strive for improvement.

Leaders must have the tools to address poor performers, acknowledge high performers, document these discussions AND be held accountable for doing so. There must be a consequence of employees not meeting the clear expectations of an employer at all levels.

Employees have expectations also. When they invest their time, they have expectations of being treated fairly and as a valuable member of the team. A great test of this is asking your employees if they believe their manager is "for them", "against them" or "for themselves".

Good customers and employees don't leave bad companies or tasks; they leave bad leadership. If a company constantly has employees transfer, resign or retire as a result of their treatment, leadership has failed. There is an extreme consequence to an employer or individual leader when they continuously do not meet employee expectations. It is called turnover and cost companies billions of dollars each year.

Growing companies actively pursue improvement. Stagnant companies remain in the maintenance mode. When high expectations of the employer and employee are both met; money and time are no longer spent, they are invested. When this occurs, you are leading like you own it and your competitors will not stand a chance.

Chapter 26. Not On My Watch!

I've heard this statement most of my life. Most of the times, it was said in a joking manner but after some quick research and thought, I believe it should apply to every manager and supervisor in every company, organization, government agency and crew. As I typed away, I also realized the need in this country for every leader, politician, parent and voter to immediately adopt "Not On My Watch" as their battle cry.

Let me share what I discovered as the origin of "Not On My Watch":

It's nautical, rather than military, and it doesn't come from any specific incident but from the nature of command on board ship. On board a ship the day and night are divided into "watches" (which are like shifts in industry) and the officers take turns to be "officer of the watch", i.e. on duty and in charge. On a warship these will usually be lieutenants. On a merchant vessel, it will be the mates.

In small vessels (gunboats etc) more junior people also get to do this duty; to be a "watch-keeping officer" for a petty officer entails serious status, because it involves taking responsibility for the whole ship and its crew. Everything that happens "on your watch" is your responsibility. If any accident or wrongdoing occurs, it's a bad mark against you even if you didn't have anything directly to do with it, because you were in charge and should have stopped it from happening.

This chapter is not about politics; it's about leadership. We have recently heard many discussions of a government shut-down, partial shut-down or whatever you want to call it. I love acronyms, so I will refer to the shut-down as the PDOI (Public Display Of Incompetence). If the PDOI does occur, it will not occur all of a sudden. It will gradually occur over months and years. It is no different than one spouse finally leaving the other. There is a defined date they physically left, but their heart left months or possibly years ago.

Back to the discussion of the PDOI. The parties were discussing the fact that this was not the first PDOI. It had occurred multiple times in the past. Keep in mind, the PDOI did not immediately financially impact the parties holding this discussion.

From an outsider's viewpoint, it appeared since it had occurred in the past, it was no big deal. Then it hit me like that old ton of bricks that seems to be suspended over each one of us. Our ability to listen and comprehend determines whether that ton of bricks is suspended with chains or a piece of six pound test fishing line. There are some people that their ton of bricks never falls. They never get it.

Here was my ton of bricks. We have become so used to mediocre and poor performance, it has become the norm. We have lost our ability to be shocked at what others do and ashamed of what we do. In all my years in corporate America, I can't even imagine going to the person that controlled my pay check and saying "we are shutting down, the other department won't do what I want". If I had said that, those words would be classified as my last words as an employee.

In a company, it happens on "Your Watch" when you ignore poor performers and don't use the leadership tools available to grow and develop others.

Du Du, Du Du Du Du. Recognize that tune? That is the theme to Mission Impossible. Early in each TV show and movie, we always heard these words; "Your mission, should you choose to accept it is ….". They always accepted it. It was exciting and successful.

If you have accepted a position as a manager, politician, leader, parent or voter, you have accepted a mission. The mission is to put the success of your crew, team, city, county, state, country, company, organization, government agency or child in front of your selfish choices.

As a registered voter, your mission is to become your own person, do your own research and quit voting for a party because that's what your daddy did. In case you haven't noticed, these ain't your daddy's parties but this isn't about politics, it's about leadership.

Let's revisit a sentence from above. Everything that happens "on your watch" is your responsibility. So, if any accident or wrongdoing occurs, it's a bad mark against you even if you didn't have anything directly to do with it. You were in charge and should have stopped it from happening.

Until each one of us take personal responsibility and adopt the battle cry of "Not On My Watch", our team, crew, company, government agency, city, county, state, country, family, health, finances and marriages are in jeopardy of a lot of bad marks.

If you consistently improve and "get better", your battle cry will always be "Not On My Watch!"

Chapter 27. Dear Boss,

So many managers and supervisors are promoted from within and are not provided the basics of producing results through others. When I was a telephone technician, I installed and repaired phones. I was held to a level of accountability and was able to meet these expectations with MY hands.

After my promotion, I was held to the same level of accountability but had to achieve this with the hands of OTHERS. Our responsibility as a leader can be summed up in this letter:

Dear Boss,

"I am your team member. I am what separates your company, organization, government agency or crew from any other. You will either grow and improve with me or maintain and go out of business with me. My family and I are counting on you to grow and improve.

You have the potential to be one of the most influential people in my life. You will either work to make a check or make a difference.

You have the ability to make reporting to work challenging and enjoyable or a living hell for me. You will either be "For Me", "Against Me" or "For Yourself". If you are "For Me", I will walk through walls for you. If not, I will do just enough to get by or I will leave unless I am one of the five percent that are high performers even in the absence of leadership. I am every level of management and non-management.

It is your job, your responsibility to improve, develop and help me be successful. It is NOT my job to make you successful, but my success will certainly contribute to your success.

If we are to grow and improve together, three things must exist:

• Education - You must insure I have the tools and training to be successful.

• Engagement – Talk to me. Don't assume I know your expectations. This is NOT a once a year rubber stamped review or through e-mail or memo. Explain the company culture, your expectations of me, my progress, praise me, correct me and help me be successful. Let me know what role I play in the success of the business.

• Accountability – If I don't meet the standards, improve my performance or change my behavior, hold me totally accountable. You have many tools in your Leadership Tool Kit. You have performance improvement plans, different levels of discipline and if all else fails, terminations. For our sake, be consistent and use them. If you go months and years without using these tools, either your expectations are too low or YOU are not held accountable.

You probably have responsibility for a six or seven figure annual payroll. Ignoring the basic responsibilities of leadership places the livelihoods associated with that payroll at risk. Let's work together to insure the success of our organization."

Sincerely,
Your Team Member

Did you notice the letter started out, Dear Boss? You are a boss when you first arrive. You will have to establish your credibility before earning the title of Leader. Every Manager, Supervisor and Leader that consistently "gets better" can live up to this letter. Can you?

Chapter 28. We Need To Be Quicker In Growing Tired Of The Attack.

Our company is like every other company when it comes to accidents. We do everything to increase awareness but sometimes an accident occurs. When it does, there is an abundance of paperwork required. The individual must have a handwritten account of what occurred.

This is a story of a dog bite accident that occurred years ago. The employee's attempt at being very descriptive and articulate brought pleasure to hundreds.

It all began with one person reading the employee's account of the accident, whiting out the name, phoning a friend and saying these very non-productive words; "go stand by your fax machine."

I regret being a party to this years ago, but I have now justified my misuse of company time and resources by using this in an Educational manner. Here is the employee's account of this unfortunate incident;

"It was a beautiful day. I was working on a trouble ticket. I was on my knees working at the protector on the side of the house. I heard a loud rustling of leaves behind me.

I quickly turned my head. I saw a large German Shepherd approaching me at a fast rate of speed. I quickly sprang to my feet to address my attacker.

When the dog first arrived at my location, he procured my left arm and shook his head. He then unprocured my left arm and procured my right arm. He again shook his head.

He then unprocured my right arm and procured my testicles.

It was at this point; I quickly grew tired of the attack. I began to beat the dog around the head with my hands and tools. Eventually the dog unprocured my testicles. I then sought immediate medical attention."

I hate to laugh at another's pain but on that day, I did. I remember tears rolling down my cheeks. I was in a cubicle and people came running to see what was so funny.

It was like he was okay with the procuring of the arms but when the dog procured man land, then, and only then, did he quickly grow tired of the attack.

This painful event is just like life. There will be attacks. We will be at a point, coming to a point or have just left a point where we grew tired of the attack. The question is how long do we wait to do something about it.

Sadly, there are too many situations where we should grow tired of the attack, but do nothing.

In life and leadership, this will not involve a German Shepherd procuring our private parts. It doesn't involve beating an attacking animal with hand tools. Sometimes we see it coming, sometimes we are blindsided.

Most times, it involves something we are aware of but have chosen to ignore. We make the assumption it will not bite us.

Sometimes we wrongly assume it will fix itself without our involvement. Sometimes we say; "That's the way they are. Just ignore them." The attack continues.

Many times we ignore the problem because we are uncomfortable with the "courageous conversation" that is necessary to correct the problem. The attack continues.

Many times we feel guilty or embarrassed we have tolerated the attack for so long. The attack continues.

Many of us are at different points of the attack. Some are working away without any sense of danger. Some hear the leaves rustling. Some see it coming. Some already have a body part procured.

Individuals focused on getting better will minimize the times they are bitten. They are extremely aware of their surroundings. They track all items that impact their well-being and results. They take corrective action before being bitten in most cases.

No matter where we are in the process, the worst thing we can do is nothing. Draw a line in the sand and grow tired of the attack now!

Many situations can be easily solved. All it takes is planning and preparation. Many can be solved with a simple conversation of "this is where you are, this is where I need you to be, and this is what will occur if this is not achieved by this date." Many can be fixed with leadership tools such as Performance Improvement Plans or levels of discipline.

Successful leaders and individuals know everything falls into one of two categories. Those that get them closer to their goals and those that don't. Successful people grow tired of the attack quicker than unsuccessful people.

The first thing procured in this situation should have been the German Shepherd. However, had that occurred, you and I would have been robbed of this educational and very entertaining story.

The Education has just begun. Check out the next two chapters.

Chapter 29. Growing Tired Of The Attack. Part Two.

Okay, we've had a laugh and hopefully an educational moment at the expense of the dog bite victim in the previous chapter.

Let's get past the humor and back to the reportable accident. Let's get back to the preventable injury to a team member. Let's get back to the cost of the injury and possible lost time. Let's get back to this employee's negligence, the danger he placed himself in and the cost to the company.

Let's assume this technician has been trained on the safety steps necessary to enter an enclosed yard. Forget that, just interject common sense. There are many steps that could've prevented this injury. The technician chose to ignore them. The injury to the procured body parts should not be the only consequence of his actions.

There should be disciplinary action. It should not be a result of the accident. It should be a result of failing to follow known safety procedures.

Nothing says I care about you and your safety more than disciplinary action over a safety infraction before it leads to an accident.

Nothing says you and your safety mean nothing to me more than ignoring safety infractions or the continuous act of "writing them up" with no other consequences. (See the next chapter.)

Violations of safety practices cannot be ignored. They must be handled with a greater sense of urgency than a quality or productivity problem. I should have more patience with your "widgets per hour" measurement than a safety infraction that could cause loss of sight, limb or death.

I cannot imagine the guilt that would accompany ignoring or simply "writing up" a safety infraction that led to the injury or death of a team member.

Chapter 30. I've Talked To Him Eight Times - Let's Fire Him

These were the first words I heard when I picked up my phone years ago. The next words were "I've talked to him eight times, he has backed into a vehicle, we have an accident on our hands and I want to fire him.

When I finally calmed the supervisor down, I was able to get "the rest of the story". We had a parking policy of backing when we arrived instead of when we left the premise. We put a cone in front of our vehicle and proceeded to complete our work. When the work was complete, we placed the cone back on the vehicle and pulled out. Sounds simple doesn't it.

Evidently it wasn't simple for one of our team members. I requested the documentation from the supervisor. He faxed me a sheet of paper and sure enough, it said "talked to John Doe about his parking." It had eight entries with dates in the last twelve months listed down the page.

After reviewing the document, I contacted the supervisor. He saw my caller ID and answered with "are you ready to fire him?" I said I had a few more questions.

The first question was when you observed him parked incorrectly, did you have him park correctly before you left the job site. The answer was no; I just told him to park correctly in the future. I told him I was "writing him up".

My next question was with eight cases of violating our safety policy, what level of discipline was the employee currently on? I was informed he was on no level of discipline but he had talked to him eight times and he should be fired. This was well before Dr. Phil, and I asked the supervisor, how that talking thing was working for him?

I finally told the supervisor I was considering termination, but I was considering terminating him for not using our disciplinary plan, especially on safety infractions. The line got very quiet. I put him at ease with a different plan.

No one would be terminated. The employee would be placed on level one of our disciplinary plan. He would be placed on level one of the discipline plan not for the accident, but for the violation of our safety policy. He would be informed future occurrences of this nature would result in higher levels of discipline.

I explained to the supervisor if we had begun this process after the first infraction, the team member would have either corrected the problem or would have been dismissed. We only have three levels of discipline, and I'm not a fan of using all three with safety violations.

I explained to the supervisor if the accident had been more serious than a bent fender, his documentation could lead to a bigger check for the accident victim. His documentation showed we talked the talk, but we didn't take safety seriously.

We also discussed the possibility of the infraction involving the failure to wear safety glasses. If the scenario played out the same, he could have been calling the employee's wife to the hospital instead of calling me to terminate someone.

This situation was a great opportunity to ask the question; do you want to terminate him for what he has done or for what you have not done?

You see, what happened here is a manager with an unblemished safety record wanting to go from zero to dismissal because of a safety infraction that had been tolerated eight times in the past. This occurs when emotions replace good judgment.

Chapter 31. GPS In The Company Vehicle, Friend Or Foe? You Choose!

Prior to writing this book, I have been fortunate enough to have many attendees in my supervisor/manager/leadership seminar. I've had a great time and have been humbled by the feedback sheets. Hopefully, I've shared some leadership and life lessons that will assist the attendees.

A few of the attendees have recently added GPS monitoring to company vehicles. The comments and attitudes have been mixed and remember; these were managers. I remember the pain of change associated with this transition years ago. I know the ONLY person that looks forward to change is a baby with a wet diaper. Most of us are resistant to change.

After my personal flashbacks of GPS implementation, I decided to share our experiences with GPS from years ago. Hopefully, this will let others learn from our experience.

First let me share how it was put into perspective for me years ago by another manager. I was visiting with a manager of a group of Service Representatives. I shared with her the complaints we were receiving from managers and technicians about GPS on their company vehicles.

She shared the growing pains experienced when they began monitoring and recording incoming calls to their bureau years ago. They experienced an immediate surge in customer satisfaction after implementation. She referred to it as the policeman in the rear view mirror of customer satisfaction.

Did monitoring and recording the calls make the customer happier? No, it changed the behavior of our customer contact employees which resulted in more satisfied customers. She did imply the Service Reps would not be a very sympathetic ear for our managers and technicians complaining about GPS.

I'd never thought of those items, but she was right. We all seem to default to issues that impact us and forget about others. We've all had things during our life that "kept us honest" and sometimes we migrate toward the negative instead of the positive.

How did they catch speeders before radar? It's common knowledge the best speed control device ever created was a police car in our rear view mirror. In my HR position, I knew many things I said would be written or recorded. It made me better. It held me accountable. Did I like it? No, but it came with the job, and if I did or said the right thing, it didn't matter.

When we first implemented GPS, there was an immediate decrease in fuel cost and increase in productivity. Why? Did that little transmitter change the fuel efficiency of our vehicles and suddenly allow out technicians to be able to get another .5 job in a day? No. It changed behavior. It changed a culture allowed by leadership in some areas.

Note: Why did some crews have huge improvements in productivity while other crews experienced minimal improvement? This was another example of when the tide goes out, you see who is skinny dipping. You see who is "running a tight ship," who is "leading like they own it," who has been saying "not on my watch" and who just shows up and says "whatever."

It changed a culture that was present when a group of technicians decided it was acceptable to drive in every day for a noon poker game and not view this as stealing time and resources. (See the chapter on the poker game culture.)

As I thought back to our implementation years ago, there were four categories of team members; two management and two non-management. Since I now cover the difference in boss employee thinking and the Leader Owner Mindset, I will use those categories:

Management

Leader Owner Mindset – This category viewed GPS as a tool to improve our dispatching process, improve efficiency, reduce cost, become more competitive in the marketplace and preserve livelihoods. They didn't need GPS to "catch employees doing something wrong" because they visited their team enough on the job to know who abused their vehicular freedom. They saw this as nothing more than a tool to improve.

This group realized the company did not and would not spend this type of money to catch someone in the wrong. That capability has been there forever though monitoring performance and regular job visits. Managers that built strong, improving teams had already corrected problems of vehicle abuse by using other leadership tools. They saw increased efficiency as increased profitability and job security. GPS was welcomed by this group, complimented what they were already doing and as a result, the negative reaction of their team was minimized.

Boss Employee Thinkers – This category of managers saw GPS as big brother watching and a mechanized tool to catch employees doing something wrong. They saw it as a "Gotcha." They were angry about it being on their vehicle and saw it as a lack of trust. They abused the new tool by using it as the dominant tool to correct and discipline team members. No transition period was given. They focused on the negatives and exceptions instead of the positives. As a result of this mindset, the negative reaction of their team lived on and on.

Non-Management

Leading Without The Title Attitude – Hey, if GPS kept them from being sent all over the world during the day and can get them off on time to see their child's athletic event; they were all for it. They had enough confidence in the leadership of this company to believe they wouldn't spend the money on GPS if there weren't a return on the investment.

They loved what they did and the freedom to be outside instead of being cooped in an office all day. They had the attitude if they wanted to see where I am, that's okay with me because, during the time they are looking, they are paying me to do a job. They didn't see it any different than their supervisor showing up at a job site. Plus, they felt if it made us more competitive and improved their efficiency, that would increase profits and protect their job.

Employee Attitude – GPS is just another way to catch employees doing the wrong thing and fire them. It's just another way for Big Brother to cut into my freedom because they don't trust me. So what if I had to go out of my route to take care of personal business during the day. I give them more in eight hours than some do. So what if I'm wasting time or company resources. Everyone does it.

You have just witnessed examples of the different mindsets of management and non-management. These mindsets didn't surface with the implementation of GPS. These mindsets exist today and will become more noticeable at any hint of change.

GPS is no different than any other efficiency tool or technology. It is neither good nor evil. It can be used in a positive or negative manner. It can be used with other leadership tools such as communication of expectations, feedback, praise and levels of discipline if necessary or it can also be used as another hammer by the boss-employee mindset.

Looking back on it, years ago we spent too much time complaining and focusing on what we perceived as a lack of trust. Perception is very strong, and if there was a lack of trust, it existed well before GPS. Normally this is caused by a lack of engagement and communication. This time wasted could've been better spent focusing on our internal and external customers.

In retrospect, there were two totally different attitudes in management and non-management and here is the most wonderful thing; we were allowed to pick our group. How we look at all company decisions is a choice. It is determined totally by the attitude we choose to have. Come to think of it, forget GPS, life is that way also.

GPS certainly would've stopped us from driving in from all locations for our noon poker game when I was a technician and a follower. Honestly though, in an organization that weighs the impact of all choices against customer service and profitability, that poker game would've never started. That is the Leader Owner Mindset.

Chapter 32. Show me on paper what you are doing to improve your team.

Wow! What a simple, powerful, profitable and seldom used request.

As a young, three day tenured supervisor, I didn't know how to respond to this request from my leader. I was relieved when I learned he didn't expect me to respond now, but he did take the time to train me on how to fulfill that request in the future.

He discussed tools such as written performance improvement plans, different levels of discipline, praise, progress reports, feedback, listening, goals and objectives and terminations. He provided guidance on how and when to use each.

He shared with a 24-year-old, new supervisor if I can respond to that request at any time, my team will always be improving, growing and developing, not just maintaining.

He assured me he would periodically request that information. He also advised me that in my career as a leader, if I constantly looked at ways to improve my team and have it documented, I would be among a small percentage of supervisors and managers that are intentional about improvement.

He strongly suggested I be able to provide this documentation, EVEN WHEN NOT REQUESTED OR REQUIRED. He stated this would put me in an even smaller percentage.

He left me with this statement, "Supervisors Supervise, Managers Manage but True Leaders Improve." Little did I know it would be included in a book nearly four decades later. The advice is timeless.

Through the years, I have always had some form of this in place. It is another example of the influence my leaders and mentors have on my Leadership Seminar and this book. The more I think about it, why would a leader not request what improvements have occurred in your team? This request assures accountability and improvement.

In fact, when thinking back, he laid the foundation for my Leadership Seminar and Keynote Presentation with showing me the importance of Education, Engagement and Accountability in that session.

As I reflect back on that 35 year-old conversation, here is another way to look at it: If you are not willing to Improve, Educate, Engage and hold your team Accountable, you might as well put that "Our Employees Are Our Greatest Asset!" poster in the trash. After all, the ONLY thing your competition does not have access to, are your employees.

What do you think of this request on a regular basis? Could you provide this information? Show me on paper what you are doing to improve your team.

Chapter 33. How To Poorly Impersonate A Supervisor.

I was a new supervisor. There were a little over three months under my belt. Through a recent interaction with a corporate attorney, I had learned, "If it's not written, it didn't occur". There had been no meetings where "Courageous Conversation" was required. That was about to change.

In the past month, Jane, (not her real name to protect the absent), was absent on two separate days. She was late a week earlier and again that day. My inexperience had already waited longer than I should.

I planned the implementation of my first performance improvement plan for tomorrow morning. I was totally prepared. At least I thought I was prepared.

The next morning, I requested Jane come by my office before leaving for the day. She came in and sat down. She had no idea of the amount of supervision, management and leadership about to come her way.

No, wait. It was me that had no idea of what was coming.

I began to discuss her attendance and punctuality of the last month. I covered the dates of the occurrences.

I had my mental leadership toolbox open. I was reaching in for the first time. I was pulling out my first performance improvement plan and then it happened. Not only did it happen, I didn't know which leadership tool to use to stop it.

What happened? First it was a few tears. Then it was a flood of tears with sobbing. I then shifted from my role as a supervisor to a role I was even more unqualified for, a counselor.

I asked what was wrong? I moved from behind the desk. (I learned later these types of meetings were better conducted on the same side of the desk or table.) I tried to comfort her as her story, and the sobbing continued.

As the crying slowed and eventually stopped, I wished her well, told her to have a good day and hoped her situation at home improved.

She left my office, got into her company truck and drove off. Instead of leaving with a performance improvement plan from a leader, she left with a goodbye wave from a guy impersonating a supervisor.

I did not do these but since we are covering what NOT to do; let's go ahead and throw in a hug, a kiss on the cheek and a swat on the behind as you say everything will be okay. Hey, why not cover all the wrong bases and invite her out for a drink after work. Then you can see if your ignorant self can offer any words of encouragement on her personal problems.

Back to the true story.

I walked into my office, and it hit me. What just happened? I felt like that one person they always find for the television interview after a tornado.

Shazam. I didn't even know it was coming. All of a sudden, there were tears and sobbing, and a big storm of emotions, a story and all of a sudden it was gone. I didn't know what hit me.

I'm not saying she wasn't under a lot of stress. I'm not saying the emotions were an act. I'm not saying she intended to play me, but if she did, she did a masterful job. She played me like a skilled violinist would play a Stradivarius.

I drove to my manager's office. I ran the entire scenario by him and asked for advice. I'm so thankful he held the laughter at least until I left. He asked if I wanted him to meet me at my office the next morning and show me how he would handle the situation. I said no, I just wanted some guidance.

I don't care what level we achieve or the tenure we acquire, we can always benefit from guidance. It is now referred to as coaching. I sought coaching that day and have sought it many times since then.

The next day came, and I asked Jane back into my office. I began the discussion about absence and punctuality again. Again, the tears began to flow. I got up, said I would step outside for a few minutes while she composed herself, and I would return.

I returned, began the discussion and the tears began again. I excused myself again.

In total, I excused myself three times before we were able to continue and conclude the meeting. Jane was placed on a performance improvement plan, and I had my first of many Courageous Conversations that would occur in my career.

I had used one of the tools in the Leadership Toolkit. I had done what they were paying me to do. When my manager asked me what I was doing to improve my team, I had an example.

Before I leave this chapter, I want to include a couple of side notes. I remained in this supervisor position for two years. When I left, Jane had not missed a day nor had been late since our meeting. Engagement and Accountability work.

This meeting had taken place years before I knew anything about an Employee Assistance Program. When this became available, I became an immediate fan.

I didn't know what caused her performance and behavior problems. Honestly, it wasn't my job to know or solve her personal problems. I was responsible for results. I had to allow a reasonable time for correction and handle the problem accordingly.

When we first had access to EAP, it was such a relief for our team members to have access to professionals. Personal problems frequently appear at work as performance or behavior problems. If you have access to EAP, use it. If not, talk to your HR department about establishing EAP as part of your benefits plan.

This is my EAP speech I used at the first glimmer of a performance or behavior problem; I don't know if there are outside factors impacting your ability to effectively perform your job, but if this is a possibility, please take advantage of our EAP program.

If EAP is not available, I would use this statement; I don't know if there are any outside factors impacting your ability to effectively perform your job, but if this is a possibility, you may want to seek outside assistance.

Chapter 34. How To Fix Most Performance Problems.

There is so much in this book about the leadership tools such as Performance Improvement Plans and levels of discipline. These are available and necessary at times, but I want to make you aware of what I've found to correct most performance and behavior problems. It is a simple, documented discussion.

This is where you make someone aware of a potential or current problem. You say something like; "this is where you are, this is where we need you to be, and this is what will occur if you cannot achieve this. How can I help?

Never attack them personally or undermine their self-worth. Focus on results, not personalities or emotions.

You will be amazed at the success you will have just by bringing awareness to the performance or behavior problem. In most cases, they already knew. Now they know you know. You have now placed a consequence on their failure to meet expectations or future occurrences.

Note: Before you go into any discussion of performance problems, ask yourself these three questions;

1. What do I want for the team member?

2. What do I want for me?

3. What do I want for the relationship?

Of course, you want success for the team member. That ultimately leads to success for you. You must conduct the meeting in a respectful manner that does not damage the long-term working relationship.

The greatest leaders are the ones that are consistent and even after a disciplinary meeting, the team member knows they care about them and their success.

Chapter 35. We Are Government! We Are Different!

I had just finished a leadership seminar with a group of government supervisors and managers. It was a great session with good interaction. I was reviewing the 20 Feedback Sheets and there it was. Among the 8's, 9's and 10's, there was a SIX! What do they mean? How dare they? Who do they think they are? I couldn't wait to read their anonymous comments.

Here is what they said: "This was good information for a "For Profit" industry but we are the government. We are different. This will not work for us. You need to learn more about your customer before you train government supervisors. We are different."

Wow! I thought "what is the best thing I can do for this organization?" My initial thought was to hand the form to the leader of this organization for handwriting analysis. Once they identify the culprit, immediate termination was the best answer. This attitude is a cancer in this organization. This was an entitlement attitude at its worst.

I quickly squelched those thoughts. This was not the normal mindset but this person believes this.

How can:

Educating each team member to do their job, regularly communicating expectations, progress, praise, need for improvement and holding ALL team members accountable NOT apply to ANY organization?

I don't care whether you are private or public sector. I don't care if your revenue comes from selling widgets, services, taxes, donations or grants. Not applying the basics of leadership skills leads to cutbacks, layoffs and closures.

Show me your team member training records. Show me documentation of discussions of expectations, progress and/or praise. Show me the number of team members placed on performance improvement plans, levels of discipline or terminated. Show me these things and I can tell how efficient and profitable you are. I can see your commitment to customer service. I can predict the morale of your employees. I can predict all of this by your level of Education, Engagement and Accountability.

My dilemma was how can I learn from this comment sheet and share something in the future that could change this attitude?

This is what I decided to do. In my next seminar with government supervisors and managers, I shared that feedback sheet. I then asked the group this question; what are you currently doing that could not be contracted or outsourced? The attorneys taught me well. Never ask a question if you don't already know the answer. I waited for a response. After nearly a minute of silence and looking at each other, one person finally spoke up and gave the correct answer; which was "nothing".

I explained this is the attitude we must have. Years ago, when I finally had my feet on the ground in my HR position, I met with my team, and discussed that possibility. We had to make ourselves so valuable, so easy to do business with, that no one ever considered outsourcing or contracting out our services. Every leader should do the same.

We should never use outsourcing or contracting as a threat or keep team members in fear of the possibility. The flip side is no organization should operate in a manner where team members believe they can perform at a mediocre level and retain employment. Customers can not be retained through mediocrity so neither should employment. That is a Lack Of Leadership and is NOT LOL (Laugh Out Loud). It doesn't matter what sector you come from or if your revenue comes from cash, credit cards, donations or taxes.

FYI: The term "good enough for government work" came about in the 1940's during WWII. Every plane, vehicle or tank that came off the line had to be of the best quality because it was going to war. A brother, father or loved one may be depending on the quality. I've asked every seminar of government managers if that statement still means the same today? Normally there is laughter. It didn't change overnight. It changed gradually with every absence of accountability. The lack of accountability also applies to the private sector. The absence of Engagement and Accountability closes more doors than the economy.

The Power Of Better works in the public AND private sectors. Education, Engagement and Accountability work in both sectors.

Chapter 36. Your First Leader

In 2013, I was fortunate enough to speak to a group of college students working on an organization's summer intern program. Later in the week I conducted a local seminar attended by managers and supervisors with decades of management experience. What a wide gap in leadership and life experiences.

These young interns had anywhere from six months to two years of college remaining. At the end of college, they will seek employment. When asked how many wanted to pursue a position of leadership, all hands were raised.

I truly believe the most important leader we will all experience is the first one. They can place you years ahead or years behind other leaders in your first six months as a new leader. This can be overcome later in a career but why not start out ahead instead of catching up.

If you have read any of our material, you know we believe in two mindsets of leadership: the boss-employee and the Leader Owner Mindset. My hope is each one of these interns has the opportunity to work initially with a strong Leader Owner Mindset Leader.

Here is how I hope it plays out for each intern:

Education: Each new leader is given the tools and training to be successful in their position. They must be familiar with every leadership tool available. These include but are not limited to: Training, Establishment of KRA's (Key Result Areas), Praise, Communication, Listening Skills, Feedback, Constructive Criticism, Performance Improvement Plans, Different Levels of Discipline and Termination.

Engagement: The company culture, expectations, progress, suggestions for improvement and praise are discussed and documented with the new leader on a regular basis. If this takes place and is also required of the new leader with their team, it will become a habit carried through a career. If not required, it will also be a habit carried through a career.

Accountability: After Education and Engagement, the new leader must be held totally Accountable for results. If total Accountability is required, it will be passed through every level of the organization.

We have a few simple questions that determine the level of Education, Engagement and Accountability in an organization.

1. Name one example of improved profitability or customer service as a result of your intentional actions in the past 12 months. _____ (Ability to answer quickly determines Intentional vs. Accidental Leadership. Note: Does not include solving day to day problems.)

2. Number of hours spent in training in the past 12 months? _____ (Measures Education and Development)

3. Not counting annual reviews, how many documented one-on-one discussions of the company culture, vision, expectations, personal progress or praise have occurred in the past 12 months? _____. (Measures Engagement)

4. Number of team members placed on a performance improvement plan or level of discipline in the past 12 months? _____. (Measures Improvement and Accountability)

Improve these answers and you will improve Efficiency and Morale. My life and career would have been totally different if all my first leader expected was distributing tasks and putting out fires. I would have never led like I owned it, and you would not be reading this.

Chapter 37. What Culture Is In Your Wallet? (The Poker Game)

What cultures are present in your organization? What are your oughts and ought nots? Are some of your cultures having a negative impact on profitability and customer service? Then look in the mirror and ask why you allow these cultures to exist.

Cultures exist in every organization. Even the absence of a culture is a culture. Cultures will be determined by leadership from the top down or determined by team members from the bottom up. As a leader, you get to choose.

Here is a couple of examples of cultures;

In the mid-60s, my grandmother and I left the farm one day and rode to town to get a sack of hamburgers. I was probably 12 years old, and it was summer because I was out of school. I finished my sack on the 12-mile trip back to the farm and threw my sack and bottle out the window.

I know my grandmother was older, but I do not believe her reactions were that slow. I believe she watched the odometer, drove a half mile and pulled over on the side of the road. She didn't back up, she stopped. She then instructed me to go back and get the sack and bottle. She then informed me, we do not litter.

I remember making the walk to retrieve the sack and bottle in mid-July. When I returned, she again informed me we do not litter. There are many more candles on my birthday cake now but I can be on a deserted country road in the middle of the night and I will not throw trash out of the vehicle. Why? Because my grandmother established a culture with me on that hot summer day. It has remained with me. There will never be a need for retraining.

Let me share a work-related culture I'm not proud of. When I was a young technician and a follower, my crew began a culture. We decided to drive from where ever we were to meet at the storeroom at noon to play poker every day. This was in the 70's and gas was much cheaper then, but we started a bad culture. We all received one hour for lunch, but lunch was from when we finished a job until we arrived at the next job. The entire crew abused this privilege by driving from all over the territory to play poker at noon.

What should have happened didn't. Our manager should have stopped this practice immediately, but didn't. This practice continued for weeks until it was finally stopped. Our manager did not stop it; it was stopped by one of our senior crew members.

One day he told us we were stealing from our company. What we were doing was having a negative impact on profitability and customer service. No one could disagree with him, and no one argued. He then stated in Hope, Arkansas, Southwestern Bell was not the telephone company. The telephone company in Hope, Arkansas was the seven crew members sitting around that table.

The culture of playing poker at noon was eliminated that day. It should never have begun. It started like most bad and good ideas begin. It begins with one person coming up with a good or bad idea and through either persuasion or intimidation, convinces others to go along. I was a 19-year-old follower at the time, but that is no excuse. It also showed me you do not need a title of manager or supervisor to be a leader.

Be sure and read the chapter on the line in the sand to see how to handle these situations.

If you were leading like you own it, would you allow your technicians to drive hundreds of extra miles per week to play poker?

Chapter 38. The Line In The Sand.

My farm is located on sandy land. Last year I was dragging a box blade on a road and looked behind me. There was a 50-foot line in the sand. This reminded me of so many times in my life and career where I've had to draw a line in the sand and change direction.

Many times in management, we inherit negative practices or cultures. We may have allowed those practices or cultures to continue. When we finally realize they are having a negative impact on customer service and profitability, we have to make a change. We have to stop the practice or change the culture.

Coming from a union environment I've heard these words many times; "you have already set a precedent." It took me years to realize I did not have the authority to set a precedent. Precedence should never be established if it has a negative impact on customer service or profitability.

Many times through either inheritance or allowance, I have stopped practices that had a negative impact on customer service or profitability. Doing this is very simple and involves this statement; "I realize this has been an accepted practice at this location for quite some time. I have been wrong for allowing this to continue. We can all see the negative impact this has upon customer service or profitability and effective today, this practice is no longer acceptable and will not be tolerated. Are there any questions?"

If you truly lead like you own it, you will never allow yourself to get caught up in practices that hurt customer service or profitability. In many cases, this will require a huge dose of humility when you have allowed the practice to continue under your leadership. Some cases may involve you eating crow, but I have found through the years crow is best eaten when warm. Not when it's cold and crusty.

Chapter 39. Why Do You Do What You Do?

A few years ago I was visiting someone in a hospital. I ran into a friend in the hall, and we stopped to visit. This friend knew I retired, but they also knew I was teaching leadership programs and doing keynote presentations. They asked me why I was doing the leadership training when I was retired? She said when you retire, you're supposed to retire.

It seemed my friend wanted an answer, so I decided to answer that question more for myself than for them.

This is why I do what I do;

1. I love it. I love speaking, teaching and sharing the lessons of the great leaders and mentors in my life.

2. Leadership, speaking and human resources have been a major part of my life for many decades, and I'm good at it.

3. It's my way of giving back and making a contribution.

4. I struggled with the fourth reason but finally came up with it; they give me money.

I then turned the tables. I asked her; isn't that why you do what you do? I received a deer in the headlights look from her until she finally said yes, that is why I do what I do.

You see, I have done some things in my life for only the money. I am totally convinced if I do it for the money only, it's unlikely that I enjoy what I do. If I don't enjoy what I do, it's unlikely I will be good at it. If I'm not good at it, it's highly unlikely I'm making much of a contribution to the organization or the world.

Note: Loving what I do is a transition and choice. You don't start out loving it. You probably start out because of the money. Then you decide to become good and then better at it. You begin to make a contribution and then all of the sudden, you make the decision to enjoy what you do.

Another way of looking at it could be your employer doesn't care if you love it or not. They are more interested in your contribution and results in exchange for compensation.

In 2014, another way of looking at this hit me. I had the most wonderful vacation with all of my family under one roof in a condo in Orange Beach, Alabama. We had a phenomenal time. I saw both of my daughters parasail again. I witnessed both of my grandson's parasail for the first time. The laughter was continuous and contagious.

As I watched them having fun, it hit me. This is my passion. Making memories with my family and friends is where my passion lies. The speaking and training finances my passion. I am very fortunate I enjoy the speaking and training. To do the speaking and training, I must do the marketing which is something I do not enjoy.

So here's the way I look at it; to enjoy my passion which is making memories with family and friends, I must finance it by doing something that fortunately, I enjoy. To do what I enjoy which finances my passion, I must do what I don't enjoy which is marketing.

I guess you can say that to get to the beach, I must do something I don't enjoy, which is marketing. I must do what I don't enjoy to do what I enjoy, which is speaking and educating.

Every job has these unpleasant tasks. The quicker you place the focus on what you enjoy, the quicker your enjoyment and contribution will increase.

We all must be doing something. Even if it's not something you enjoy as much as I enjoy speaking and teaching, why not decide to be excellent at it. That's why I devote hundreds of hours and thousands of dollars in getting better at what I do. I want to be better at financing my passion by bringing more value to my customers. It's impossible to go wrong by bringing more value to your customers.

Many of you may not be in your "dream job." What is your passion? Is it hunting, fishing, golf or like me, making memories with your family and friends? Why not decide to be excellent at what you do so it can finance your passion. Get better at what you do. I promise it will become more enjoyable.

Do not fall prey to the motivational speakers that tell you to do what you love and you'll never have to work another day in your life. This is a crock.

I had a great career and enjoyed every position I held, but I honestly cannot say I'd dreamed about walking through water up to my chest to climb a telephone pole to restore service. I did not dream of being on a telephone pole in freezing weather during a sleet storm. I did not even dream about being a human resources manager and hearing grievances, arbitrations, EEOC complaints, lawsuits or dealing with violence in the workplace, but I decided to be good at it. So can you. That is leading like you own it.

P.S. A few years ago at Christmas, the entire family was again under one roof. I sat and listened. I can't count the times I heard, "Dad or Papaw, remember when we did this?" Or "Dad or Papaw, remember when we went there?" Not once did I hear, "Dad or Papaw, remember when we bought _____?" It's not about things. It's about going places, doing things together and making memories.

Whatever you do, do not miss the chapter on the bucket story. It changed my priorities, and I have shared it with thousands.

Chapter 40. The Bucket Story

In 1989, on my first day in my human resources position, I was given an assignment. This assignment was to form a committee with all the other personnel managers in the company. My manager wanted to insure we were consistent across the company. At the time, I did not see the huge impact this would have on my life, career and friendships.

There were 16 of us that handled personnel duties for our department across the company. We met in Dallas, elected a chairman (not me because I didn't have a clue) and continued to meet quarterly for many years. This committee allowed me to establish friendships and tap into mentors that had been in personnel for many years. I cannot describe the impact of this committee on both my professional and personal life. If you have peers that do what you do, believe me, everyone benefits when experiences are combined and shared.

One of the gentlemen in the personnel committee was Dick Welt from Kansas City. He had years of experience in personnel. I quickly grabbed his coat tail and used him as a mentor and resource.

One night while having dinner in St. Louis, Missouri, Dick asked the age of my daughters. They were probably 12 and 14 or 13 and 15 at the time. He said I've noticed you have been putting in a lot of hours by the weekend and late-night voice mails. (At this time in my life and career, I was in the mode of a 65-75 hour, self-imposed work week.)

He said, don't get me wrong; I'm not picking them up late at night or on the weekends, but I need to share the bucket story with you.

He said when he was first promoted, he attended a seminar. At the door was a table, two buckets and an instruction card. He had to put his finger in the first bucket filled with water, pull out his finger, dry his hand and move to the second bucket. He then had to place his finger in the second bucket filled with sand or silt, pull out his finger, wipe it off and sit down.

When the instructor arrived in the class, he said you're probably wondering about those two buckets at the back of the room. The first bucket, you stick your finger down in the water, you occupy space, you remove your finger, and the water fills back in immediately. It is just like you were never there. I hate to admit it, but that's your company. If you leave tomorrow, they will probably fill your vacancy and it will quickly be like you were never there.

The second bucket, when you stick your finger in the sand or silt, you also occupy space but when you remove your finger, you leave a void. Now over time, the sand or silt will shift around and fill in but it takes a long time. This is your family.

Friends, Dick Welt could not have hit me in the head with a brick and had any more impact on me. He made me realize how I had my priorities out of order. After sharing the story, he didn't criticize or condemn me, he changed the subject. There is an old cliché when the student is ready, the teacher will appear. I was ready that night in St. Louis, and the teacher appeared as my friend and mentor, Dick Welt.

I would love to say I immediately changed my work week to 40 hours but no, I didn't. However, I did begin making gradual changes as a direct result of The Bucket Story. One of the changes is shared below.

March 13, 1994 was a normal Sunday at the Gilbert household. Sandy got up and got the girls ready for church. I got up and went to work. Before you judge me, I always took off early on Sunday, somewhere around 4:00PM. But this Sunday was different. This Sunday was four days after Dick had shared the bucket story with me.

I arrived at the office between 8:30 and 9:00AM. It didn't hit me for an hour but when it did, I couldn't shake it. There it was. The bucket story. It seemed I couldn't work for more than 30 minutes without the bucket story surfacing in my mind. Finally, at 1 PM I'd had enough. I locked up and headed home.

At that time, my oldest daughter, Amber, and I had a running battle on who could make the most consecutive free throws. Whenever a new record was set, I scratched the date, the number of consecutive free throws and the initials of the record holder on the goal post in our driveway. We had started with low numbers, and I currently held the record of 15 consecutive free throws. This was really bugging Amber because she was very competitive.

As I pulled into my street, I noticed Amber on the free-throw line. I knew she was going for my record. I parked on the street, walked over to the driveway and began throwing the ball back. In the next 15 minutes, I witnessed my daughter make 32 consecutive free throws.

I retrieved the screwdriver, scratched the new record on the goal post and immediately announced my retirement from future free throw competitions. I felt youth would continue to hold that record. I would stick to playing HORSE, which I also seldom won.

Here's what scares me absolutely to death. What would have happened if Dick Welt had not cared enough about me to share the bucket story? It is very possible, no, it is probable, I would have been notified by an excited phone call or I would've left my office at my normal Sunday time of 4 PM.

I would have driven into my driveway and would have been greeted with the excitement of my wife and two daughters screaming "Amber made 32 consecutive free throws. You need to scratch it on the goal post." It would not have been the same. I am so thankful I witnessed the breaking of my record. I attribute my presence at this family memory to a story I needed to hear from a friend and mentor.

I have since shared this story with thousands. I have seen eyes begin to sweat as I share it (eyes sweating is a manly way of saying I wept like a small child.) I have been humbled by the feedback on this story. I will continue to share this story as long as I speak and teach. Future Volumes of "The Power Of Better" series will also contain the bucket story because I think it is important everyone hear it and take an inward look at their priorities.

We can always make more money, but time is a finite resource. Use it like you own it.

Chapter 41. My Greatest HR Challenge!

I want to share one of my greatest challenges as a Human Resources Manager. It didn't occur in front of an attorney, arbitrator, union president or one of my managers. It occurred in front of my then, 13-year-old, favorite youngest daughter.

Both of my daughters on many occasions have said, "Dad, leave that HR stuff at work. We are your daughters, not your employees."

One Christmas, I decided to give both daughters a checking account. That was the HR Manager/Dad version of compensation.

Next I prepared a list of duties to be completed each week. That was the HR Manager/Dad version of a job description. Upon completion, each Friday I would deposit three dollars into my youngest daughter's account, and five dollars into my oldest daughter's account. Friday was payday!

As usual, we had a great Christmas but I could tell something was bothering my youngest daughter. When I asked what was wrong, that is where the challenge began. She stated she had looked at her list of duties, and it was the same as her older sister. I agreed. I didn't even recognize it but this was the bait.

She then asked why she received three dollars and her sister received five dollars. I responded and even as highly trained as I was, I didn't see it coming. I said "normally the older child receives the larger allowance." Have you ever mistakenly squeezed a tube of toothpaste? That's how I immediately felt when those words came out. I couldn't put them back.

I've been on the witness stand a few times, and there are two things you do not want to occur. One is you do not want to be caught in a lie, and the other is to be caught in ignorance. After my last statement, I was caught in ignorance, and all I could hope for was mercy. It didn't happen.

My daughter then had a question for me. She asked, "At SW Bell, if you hired two people to do the same job, one was 26 years old, and the other was 28 years old, would you pay the 28 year old more money just because she was older?" She had me. Deer in the headlights look comes to mind.

I mentally explored my options:

Option 1. I could use the tactics of the generation before me. I could state I was the father, it was my plan, and that is how it will be. I didn't like being on the other side of that plan when I was younger, so I decided against that one.

Option 2. This was the option I chose: I looked my daughter right in the eyes and stated, Autumn; you have just effectively argued equal pay for equal work with your Dad/HR Manager and effective immediately you will receive a two dollar retroactive increase in compensation. We hugged and went on with Christmas.

I received a suggestion from a manager after telling this story at a meeting. He stated I could've scratched through one of the tasks on my youngest daughters list and made them different. I thanked him for that suggestion. I'm glad I didn't think of that one. It violated my treat others like I would like to be treated rule.

The moral of this story is we all make mistakes. The best solution if you mess up is to fess up, fix it and move on. Humility and confidence CAN and MUST co-exist in the heart of a great leader or parent. I did the best thing in this situation. When you are looking long term (NOT a rental car), doing the right thing is always the best answer.

Chapter 42. Find A Way To Say Yes To Your Customers.

I'm writing this chapter in a condo in the mountains of Arkansas. I rented a condo for a week. Since it is a timeshare organization, they normally rent Sunday through Sunday or Saturday through Saturday. Evidently the condos are not full this time of year because they're only four cars outside. Because of my schedule I had the need to stay one additional night.

After calling multiple 800 numbers and talking to many members of the NO family, I finally found Janet in the local office. She was part of the YES family. Although this was not their company policy, she found a way to help me. This resulted in additional revenue for her organization and the rental of a condo that would have been empty. She found a way to say yes.

Through this journey and conversations with the NO family, I heard these statements;

1. That's not our company policy.
2. Our system is not set up for one-night rentals.
3. If I made an exception for you, I would have to do it for everyone.
4. This is the way we've always done it.

Here's what I know. The more you make statements one through four above, the easier it is to replace you with a computer. Computers can spit out the rules, but humans can use reasoning and logic to solve problems. I was so thankful to find a person in the organization willing to find a way to say yes to a customer and additional revenue. Saying yes to reasonable customer requests protects livelihoods and displays a leading like you own it attitude.

I don't mean to upset the cat lovers, but when it comes to customer service, I want you to greet me like a dog, not like a cat. I want you to act like you're glad to see me. You don't have to wag your tail but at least make me feel you appreciate and need me. Cat-like customer service gives the message you are lucky I even acknowledge you. Never forget each customer has a first name and it is Revenue. Never forget in most cases your first name is Expense. Without Revenue, there is no need for Expense. That means you.

Always look for a way to say yes and serve your customers. That's what a Leader-Owner Mindset would do.

Chapter 43. Buy The Blanked De Blank Roses!

Do you have an empowered leadership team? Are you sure? We thought we did. We talked the talk, but we didn't walk the walk. We discovered this during a horrible customer service issue. This customer woke up 12 consecutive days without telephone service. We repaired it daily but at some point during the night, the computer would take it out of service.

Finally, after a dozen days of pitiful customer service, we found the problem. An empowered manager with a company credit card in his wallet contacted the customer to apologize for the continued disruption. He assured her the problem was corrected. He asked the customer, what can I do to make you a satisfied customer? She wanted an apology, which he had given. She wanted assurance the problem was corrected, which he had given and she wanted a dozen roses.

The empowered manager with the company credit card told the customer he would have to get back with her on the dozen roses.

He was concerned about a dozen roses appearing on a company credit card. He contacted his manager about the dozen roses. I refuse to tell you how many levels of our hierarchy were questioned before someone said "buy the **** roses." For the sake of my daughters and grandchildren, I have a eliminated the very descriptive word that preceded the word roses.

When the customer asked for the dozen roses, the empowered manager should have asked "what color and what time should we deliver them?" We learned from this example even though we talked empowerment, our managers did not feel empowered. That small twinge of fear and mistrust was still present. All that had to occur was a simple note on the receipt explaining the circumstances of the purchase.

Did this manager lead like he owned it? Absolutely not! Did he feel empowered? Absolutely not! Do you feel empowered? Does your team feel empowered? If not, it all boils down to a lack of trust. Remember in an earlier chapter, I stated "my high on trust, low on rules organization will always beat your high on rules, low on trust organization." Until trust is established, your leadership team will never lead like they own it which includes buying the roses.

I've heard discussions from attendees that wanted the manager to buy the roses but wanted to know about the expense. Why? I go back to Bob's statement; I have not been, nor do I plan on starting to scrutinize your $100 decisions.

Want to do an interesting experiment? At your next manager meeting, give the example above and ask each leader to write anonymously on an index card what they would do. Better yet, have a sheet prepared with the example and options to circle or check. Some managers may not trust you to not do a handwriting analysis on their sheet. This points to a much bigger problem. If one manager feels this way, your organization is in big trouble.

Chapter 44. Would You Buy Your Team With You As The Leader?

This is a hypothetical question. Let's assume you have a team that could stand alone. What if you could extract your team from the organization? What if you could set your team up as their own profit center with you as the leader?

What if you were given an opportunity to get a small business loan, purchase your team with you as the leader and contract back to your company? You could also market and contract to other companies as well. Your growth could be limitless.

Would you do it?

I hope your answer is yes. If your answer is no or #### NO, why do you expect your company to buy you and your team every payday? Your honest answer has just taught you so much about your character.

Do you feel "Better"?

Chapter 45. We Can't Come Over, Our Weed Eater Is Broken!

I heard a very appropriate story years ago. Bob wanted to borrow a chain saw from his neighbor, Joe. Joe said; "sorry, I can't loan it to you, we're having soup tonight." Bob asked, "what does soup have to do with loaning me your chain saw?" Joe says, "Nothing. I just don't want to loan you my chain saw and one excuse is as good as another."

Joe is right. One excuse is the same as another. The job doesn't get done.

Do you know the difference between a legitimate reason and an excuse? It all depends on whose mouth says the words. I can say the words, and it sounds like a legitimate reason coming from me. However, the same words coming from you sounds just like an excuse.

There are a few of us that help each other around our farms and homes. We have officially adopted "I can't; my weed eater is broken" as our default, one size fits all, excuse. There is no further stumbling for words and no questions asked. It is accepted you can't help. A new date is chosen or the project is started without that person.

Don't tell me you can't produce better results because of a past culture, fear of grievances or lack of upper-level support. Just tell me "my weed eater is broken." That sounds much better that, "I'm just too lazy to put forth the effort." All excuses are the same. You can have results or excuses. You choose.

Chapter 46. Pot Roast And Southwestern Bell

I heard this story in the early 80's. A husband comes home, and his wife is cooking a pot roast. He notices she has cut the pot roast in two pieces and is cooking it in two separate pans. He asks why she is doing that? She replies because her mother did it that way.

The husband calls his mother in law and asks why she cut her pot roast in two and cooked it in separate pans? She replies because her mother did it that way.

The husband calls grandmother in law and asks her the same question. She says she didn't have a pan big enough for the pot roast.

Two subsequent generations have followed a practice and never asked why. The day I heard this story, I immediately thought of my company, Southwestern Bell. We did so many things because that was the way we've always done it. I don't know if people were afraid to ask why or just didn't care.

Why are you doing some of the things you are doing at your company. Begin asking why? Do they benefit customer service, profitability or morale? Many practices can be stopped or improved, but you will never know until you ask why.

If you think all the good ideas have been taken, consider this; We put a man on the moon decades before we put wheels on a suitcase. Ask why. Why is one of the most important questions in the path to "Better".

Chapter 47. Bob's Rules.

In 1980, I reported to a new position in a the Fayetteville, Arkansas Test Center. My manager, Bob, took me to lunch on the first day. We ordered our meal and he said "I only have two rules";

Rule Number One - "If I have to do your job, I don't need you."

Rule Number Two - "I will never jump in front of you in your organization to solve a problem. I will make you aware of the problem and always give you the opportunity to solve it first. You will probably like your way of solving the problem better than mine. Welcome to the Test Center."

This was one of many great leaders that contributed to this book and my leadership seminar. I was held accountable. I've adopted "Bob's Rules" and shared them with thousands, but they are never "Greg's Rules". They belong to Bob and are worth sharing.

Chapter 48. Leadership Lessons From David Allen Coe

If you are not familiar with the country singer, David Allen Coe, take a few minutes to visit the web and check out some of his photos. You need to see a picture of a very unlikely inspiration for a leadership and life lesson. He is a scary looking dude but one of his songs inspired this chapter.

One day I was listening to an oldie country music station when one of Mr. Coe's songs began to play. After listening to the song titled "The Ride," I decided to learn to play and sing the song. A few days later I was playing around with the song. I played the first verses but after playing the chorus, the leadership and life lesson hit me. I immediately stopped playing. The last two lines of the chorus were;

He said, "Boy can you make folks feel what you feel inside? 'Cause if you're big star bound let me warn ya, it's a long, hard ride"

Boy, can you make folks feel what you feel inside? Are you passionate about what you do? Are you viewed as sincere? This line took me back years ago to a program I gave in Little Rock, Arkansas. At the end of my program, a big guy tapped me on the shoulder. He had tears streaming down his cheeks. I'll never forget his question; "are you real? Your stories touched me."

I said 10-20 years ago, I probably couldn't have passed the red face test on that question. I told him yes, I was real and my stories and lessons come from my heart. We had a good visit.

On my two hour drive back home, I couldn't get his question out of my mind. Are you real? If we are not real, there is no possible way to make folks feel what you feel inside.

Here is the smell test. Are you one person when alone with your spouse but a different person when with your spouse in a group? Are you one person when you are with your manager but another person with your peers? Are you one person with your buddies in deer camp but a different person with your church group? What if one person could see you in each of these situations? Would they know who you are? Would you appear real? If you are not consistently yourself or not real; you will have a very difficult time making folks feel what you feel inside. You will have a very difficult time convincing others you are "for them."

If you're big star bound let me warn ya it's a long hard ride. I've come to grips with not being big star bound as the song states. Some of you may already be a big star, or you are destined for stardom. I hope you are. Best wishes. Even if we are not big star bound, if we plan on doing anything meaningful or worthwhile, let me warn you, it's a long hard ride.

If you are or plan to be a successful leader, let me warn you, it's a long hard ride. If you plan on having a successful marriage, let me warn you, it's a long hard ride. If you plan on being a successful parent, let me warn you, it's a long hard ride. When these kids are teenagers, it's a long, long, long, hard ride.

I believe there is no better way to prepare for this long, hard ride than personal growth and development. What you read, watch, listen to, attend and hang around are the best ways to prepare for this long, hard ride.

Well, there you have what I consider two very good leadership and life lessons from a very unlikely source. Both of these lessons can help you "get better".

Chapter 49. Was The Title "Lying Leadership" Already Taken For Their TV Show?

I truly enjoy the TV show Undercover Boss. Because of teaching a leadership seminar, I probably enjoy it for a different reason than most. Although I enjoy the emotion, the improvements and the success stories, after watching a few episodes, I am asking myself why?

Why does a CEO/owner or upper-level leader have to lie and deceive the work force to discover problems that hurt employee morale, profitability, sustainability and customer service? Where were the front line leaders and their leaders? Where are the other layers of leadership between the owner/CEO and the employees?

On some shows, the best thing that could happen to the company was for some of the front line leaders to begin working for a competitor. Tomorrow! BUT, they didn't achieve that attitude or LOL (Lack Of Leadership) overnight. They should have already been identified, addressed, improved or set free.

Why are these problems not resolved by a front line leader that is more familiar with the job than a CEO? Are they told the rules with absolutely no input? Are the employees totally ignored? Are they not trusted or does the front line leadership just not care? Have they been beaten down where they are like a robot? Are their suggestions totally ignored until they just quit trying to improve things and just maintain?

Did the front of their tee shirt say "They Say I Am Empowered" and the back of the shirt says "But I Don't Feel Empowered"? Did Cool Hand Luke sum it up when he said "What we've got here is a failure to communicate"?

How high is the trust level where one of the "Top Dogs" lies about who they are and what they do? Is lying okay if it's for TV or "the good of the company"? Oh, please don't use the statement, "but that's business".

Why didn't the other layers of leadership recognize, address and make these changes? Why doesn't the front-line leadership change processes and improve or weed out the team members that don't contribute to the vision of a company?

What kind of vote of confidence is this to the other levels of leadership? Was this the only way to improve profitability, customer service and morale?

How does this sound? "Sir, our call may be monitored for quality assurance and I may be training our CEO who has lied to me about their identity and occupation. How may I help you?"

At my company, honesty and integrity is the number one leadership trait. It is impossible to train integrity. I struggle associating a disguise and lying with integrity.

The Undercover Boss has totally ignored "Bob's Rules". Bob's Rules have their own chapter in the book but let me recap.

In 1980, I reported to a new position in a Test Center. My manager took me to lunch on the first day. We ordered our meal, and he said "I only have two rules";

Rule Number One - "If I have to do your job, I don't need you."

Rule Number Two - "I will never jump in front of you in your organization to solve a problem. I will make you aware of the problem and always give you the opportunity to solve it first. You will probably like your way better than mine. Welcome to the Test Center."

This was one of many great leaders that contributed to this book and my leadership seminar. I was held accountable. I've adopted "Bob's Rules" and shared them with thousands, but they are never "Greg's Rules". They belong to Bob and are worth sharing. "Undercover Boss" would be unnecessary with "Bob's Rules" and accountable leadership.

There is a problem in American business. I've recently witnessed the good, bad and ugly in my town. The good was at a Chick-Fil-A. They treat you well. There are many great seeds sown in that organization. I won't share the company where I witnessed the bad and ugly. Maybe they were just having a bad day.

Wouldn't it be great for American business if every leader were a true representative of their employees, customers, leadership and the profitability of the business? The only problem is there would be no material for an "Undercover Boss" TV series. Oh well, we could read a book on leadership.

What are your thoughts? Have I overreacted? Is this okay for TV but not in real life? What if your CEO did this to you and it was not filmed for TV?

Is the concept of "Undercover Boss" an acceptable method to correct problems in an organization? Do you feel it was done to get advertising and exposure for the business? How would you feel if you were one of the employees lied to? Oh yeah, how would you feel before and after they gave you $20,000 to buy a car or help your mother? Are the gifts for the CEO to feel better about the disguise and deception?

Can a cash payout change your views on lying, deception, honesty and integrity? How much does it take? No thanks, I can get better without that.

Chapter 50. Now; It's Your Turn To Appraise Me.

I had reported directly to Bill for a month. He was in the process of going to different locations around the state to meet the team. The date of the first meeting also corresponded with the date of my annual review.

At the conclusion of the meeting, we found a private location in the hotel to cover my annual review. The review was a result of the eleven months with my previous manager and the last month with Bill.

I received a favorable review. I was pleased and looking forward to working with Bill. Upon completion of the review, something occurred I had never experienced in my 25 previous reviews. In fact, it was so unexpected, I was initially at a loss for words.

At the end of my review, Bill closed his binder and said, "It is your turn to appraise me. How am I doing as a leader?" Initially, I didn't know how far to go on this limb. After only a month and with Bill located in another state, our interaction was limited at best. I guess you could say my jury was still deliberating on whether Bill was "For Greg", "Against Greg" or "For Bill". Was he serious or was this a trap. Was it a test to see if I was a "yes person" or someone looking for a stroke of the ego. These all went quickly through my mind.

I decided to trust him. In our meeting with the team that afternoon, Bill discussed a topic I felt did not add value to a introductory meeting. I explained it could give team members a wrong first impression. I knew we had many more meetings scheduled, and this topic did not deserve time in future meetings.

After sharing this with Bill, I sat on the edge of my seat awaiting a response. This was a pivotal moment in our new working relationship. I was so relieved when he replied "you are right, I never thought of that." He thanked me for my feedback. Bill went on to be one of the many great leaders I had during my career. In fact, I have used "it's your turn to appraise me" many times in my life and career.

We may never know the true answer to this $64,000 question. If Bill had not requested feedback, would I have had the guts to correct my new leader? I'm going out on another limb and saying yes. True leaders do not want "yes people" on their team. "Yes People" will not help an organization get better.

Chapter 51. Help! I Work For An Electric Boss.

I hope this never occurs, but you need to prepare for it. At some point in your career, you may be faced with having absolutely no leadership.

You may report directly to what I call an electric boss. These bosses posses the trait of electricity in following the path of least resistance. I've always heard following the path of least resistance is what makes rivers and men crooked.

These bosses are also known as maintainers. They believe in distributing tasks and putting out fires only. They have absolutely no plan for getting better. Investing in your success is nowhere on their radar.

Many of these bosses are RIP, Retired In Place. They spend every day striving for the absolute minimum daily requirement.

You may be extremely tempted to say things like; If my boss doesn't care, why should I? Be extremely careful. Do not fall into this mode. That could be exactly where the lack of leadership you are complaining about began. This is normally a path of no return, rewards or personal satisfaction.

Continue doing the best possible job. Ask if there are ways you can increase your value to the organization. Continue to close the gap between your performance and potential. Do your job with a great attitude. These are short term solutions.

Sadly, in many cases, the only possible long-term solution is to leave. If you can transfer, do it. You may need to seek employment elsewhere. Normally these situations do not change without a change in leadership. If there seems to be a lack of accountability, it is normally the culture of the entire organization.

Learn from this experience. Vow never to become what you see as a waste of good oxygen and a paycheck.

Chapter 52. Pool Hall Leadership Lessons

If you think no good ever comes from hanging out in pool halls as a kid, think again.

As a farm kid, if I finished my farm chores early on Saturday, I would ride to Hope with my mom while she shopped for groceries. She would drop me at Jack's News Stand. I would watch as she drove off, and I would go through the alley to the pool hall. Every town had one.

The pool hall encouraged my first set of written goals at the young age of 13. After losing my hay hauling money to a group of older guys, I went home and wrote these words on the top of a piece of paper; "Guys I Will Beat In Pool." Six names were written below. Through thousands of practice hours, I gradually checked these names off. By my 18th birthday, the list was empty.

Pay attention to this lesson. This goal was accomplished by doing something different than my competition. They just played pool. I played and practiced pool. Hours and hours practicing bank shots, off the rail shots, over a ball shots. Watch what the masses are doing and do something different.

Spending this amount of time in the pool hall gave me the honor of winning an Arkansas State Eight-Ball Championship and also being part of a very dominant Pool Team from Little Rock in the 90's. I believe we still hold the record for highest finish (5th place out of over a 100 teams) by an Arkansas team in the Nationals at Las Vegas.

I learned a lot about being part of a successful team from this group of guys. Being a team player is offering encouragement after a blown game or shot. If you deserve to be on a high caliber team, you beat yourself up. You don't need that from your team mates. You need to be challenged to do your best.

Another lesson learned was curiosity didn't kill the cat, it was comparison. Quit comparing yourself to others and start comparing your performance with your potential. Work hard. Practice.

Do whatever it takes to close the gap between your performance and potential. If you are not willing to strive for improvement, or Betterment as I call it, you don't deserve to be on a team or even working for a company. Go solo. That way, you only impact the lives of you and your family; not the success or livelihoods of others.

I learned a lot about leadership from Bob, our team captain. As with any leader, they are either "For You," "Against You," or "For Themselves." Bob was definitely "For You" if you were on his team. As a result, you would walk through walls for Bob. There are only 17 vertebrae that separate a kick in the rear from a pat on the back. High performers provide their own kick in the pants. Bob knew that.

He wanted everyone to have fun but also wanted to win. When it came down to it, he had to make tough decisions on who played and who sat out. These are the same decisions any leader in a company or organization must make. If you can't make these decisions, it's simple. Get help or get out!

Last but not least, I want to address one of the most damaging statements a parent can make to a child; "it's just a game." If you are playing individual sports or work alone, I guess this attitude is acceptable. I never heard one of my team members say "it's just a game" after a personal or team member's loss. I've never heard a professional athlete say "it's just a game" after a loss. If you receive a paycheck, you are a professional.

The "it's just a game" mentality will eventually become "it's just a job" or "it's just a marriage." No offense, but if you have an "it's just a game or job" attitude, I don't want you as a team mate or a co-worker.

Yes, my ability as a pool player is probably a product of a misspent childhood. But you know what? I'm so thankful for the leadership and life lessons it provided. I'm also grateful for the relationships and camaraderie. And to think, it all began with a 12 year old kid in Hope, Arkansas throwing a dime on a pool table and telling Bull Dillard to "rack em."

Chapter 53. Lead Or Exit. A Coaching Lesson In Football, Business And Government!

As a Arkansas Razorback fan, I once went through a very painful loss at the hands of the Missouri Tigers. What made it even more painful was our quarterback played most of the fourth quarter injured. His passing inaccuracy reflected something was awry.

There were probably three different camps concerning our quarterback during the fourth quarter;

Camp One: What a brave and valiant effort by the quarterback. He has a strong heart and guts to play injured.

Camp Two: The coach should have pulled him. We won with the backup quarterback last week. It is a coach's responsibility to put us in a position to win.

Camp Three: It is the responsibility of the quarterback to put his team in a position to win. If he is too injured to fulfill this responsibility, he should ask to leave the game.

You can pick your camp but it doesn't matter. That game is over. This book is about the game in progress every day; the game of leadership in the public and private sectors. Many in positions of leadership are on the benches, in the stands or tailgating in the parking lot when they should be on the field busting it.

Years ago, one of my former HR customers requested I design a program for managers and supervisors. His exact words were; I don't want a dog and pony show, left brain, right brain, smoke and mirrors or personality profiles. I want the basics of producing results through others and I need it quickly. I want to make sure my leadership has the knowledge and tools before I hold them totally accountable.

Luckily, an attorney told me in 1978 if it is not written, it did not occur. I had kept good notes of successes, failures and what led to each through my management and HR career. I developed a program that has been shared with thousands through keynotes, breakout sessions and all day programs. The feedback has been humbling. This book is a product of those notes.

During my program, I share the leadership tools necessary to improve and develop a team. Some of these tools require having courageous conversation with poor performers. This is never fun or enjoyable but is part of being a leader. I am very honest and blunt in my program. Use the tools of a leader or GET OUT. Livelihoods are at stake.

After my first program, two supervisors approached me individually. They both said the same thing. They were not cut out to be a supervisor. They wanted to return to non-management.

The stress was greater now because the new regime was holding them totally accountable for results. This was a change from the previous leadership.

I told both of them the same answer; there is absolutely nothing wrong with what they want to do. Not everyone is cut out or wants to be a manager or supervisor. Both of them were able to return to their previous positions and were a very valuable part of the success of that organization.

Prior to that day of true confession, two things were occurring;

1. They were creating a lot of stress in their life because they were both VERY uncomfortable in having courageous conversation. They preferred the friend role.

2. They didn't want to be in leadership, so they put no effort into getting better at it.

They were performing at a level of mediocre or below.

In business, we are not talking about a football game or playing injured, there are only two camps;

Camp One: It is a leader's responsibility to put a crew, team, company or organization in a position to win. They must insure they have the Education to perform at a high level. They must Engage with the team and communicate expectations and progress. They must hold them Accountable. There may be times some team members must be pulled from the game. Livelihoods are at stake.

Camp Two: It is the responsibility of every leader to put their crew, team, company or organization in a position to win. They must get the knowledge and tools to allow winning to occur. They must USE the knowledge and tools. If they are unwilling to do this, they should ask to leave the game through reassignment or resignation. Livelihoods are at stake.

Are you putting your crew, team, company or organization in a position to win? If not, there is a lack of Education, Engagement or Accountability. Don't wait until the game is over. When there are layoffs, pay freezes, benefit reductions or closures; it is too late.

Be proactive. In the public and private sectors, business is not basketball. There is not a bench if you're having a bad day or not performing at a high level. There are no subs.

Chapter 54. Welcome Aboard. Is It Okay If I Call You At-Will?

For those of you not familiar with "At Will Employment" below is a simple explanation:

At will employment is generally described as follows: "any hiring is presumed to be 'at will'; that is, the employer is free to discharge individuals "for good cause, or bad cause, or no cause at all," and the employee is equally free to quit, strike, or otherwise cease work.

Most of my leadership and Human Resources career was in a company with a union and a labor agreement. I can make this statement without any doubt in my mind. We make the right decision more often when we know it will be challenged.

Successful leaders don't care if they are challenged. They make the right decision because it is the right thing to do, not because of a potential or assured challenge.

I'm saying these things to state I did not have total free access to Employment At Will. The only exception was with non-bargained for managers. I always knew as a manager; I was an at-will employee but when you work with great leaders, you don't live in fear of being an at-will employee.

Even though I didn't have free access to Employment At Will, I wouldn't have used it if given the opportunity. I believe it is a tool that is available and used by lazy bosses, not leaders.

I believe Employment At Will allows a boss to use personal feelings and personality conflicts to terminate an employee. It allows inconsistencies. It can allow a boss to legally play favorites. It also allows a boss to terminate an employee without using any of the leadership tools available that could have corrected a performance or behavior problem.

I have seen the career, attitude and life changing benefit of performance improvement plans and different levels of discipline.

Quick use of dismissal under Employment At Will robs an employee of an opportunity to correct the problem. If you ever have the desire to be a true leader, it could also rob you of the opportunity to make a true difference in someone's life. It robs you and the dismissed employee of "what could've been".

As the primary Human Resources contact for over 2000 team members, I have received many calls that began with, "can I fire them for this?" That is never the correct question. The correct question is "what is the right thing to do?" "Can I fire them for this" always threw up a red flag with me. It always made me think of a personality conflict or someone that wasn't brown-nosing at the same depth as other crew members.

I frequently asked this question; Do you want to terminate this employee because of what they have done or because of what you have not done? I have zero tolerance for bosses that choose termination as their first level of discipline. These are normally bosses quick with the kick in the rear but are physically unable to pat someone on the back.

FYI - There are only 17 vertebrae that separate a kick in the rear and a pat on the back but the outcome is extremely different.

I do want to clarify all of this goes out the window on cases of extreme misconduct. I will not attempt to define extreme misconduct because each organization has their own definition.

Terminations should never be a surprise. An employee should have an opportunity to correct the problem. I have found most performance and behavior problems are fixed with these two statements; Here's where you are, here's where I need you to be and here's what will occur if you are not there by this date. What can we do to get there?

In summary, I believe the Employment-At-Will Doctrine is a tool used by lazy bosses. I compare it to bankruptcy. Yes, it is legal but is it right? Does it allow you to shirk your responsibility as a true leader the same way bankruptcy allows you to shirk your responsibility as a debtor?

I feel the number one responsibility of a true leader is to develop their team members. Employment At Will allows bosses to shun that responsibility. I compare it to parenting. Our obligation as a parent is to use the parenting tools available to develop children into responsible, productive adults.

If are a parent and one of the frequent fliers of Employment-At-Will airways, your children should pray they never pass a Child At Will law. They will find themselves in the foster system at the first sign of trouble.

Except in cases of misconduct, termination should be the unpleasant final result of the unsuccessful use of every leadership tool available.

If you can't list what you did to correct the problem, I hope no one I care about ever has to work for you. In fact, I hope even the people I don't know or care about never have to work for you. Whoops! That would pretty much put you out of a job. Well, I'm sure you are aware you are an at-will employee. See Ya.

Chapter 55. Leadership And Life Lessons I Learned From My Guitar!

While setting my goals for 2015, I had a mental block. I picked up my guitar and placed the capo next to one of the frets. One string was extremely out of tune, and the song sounded horrible. I am always looking for unique methods to share life and leadership lessons, so these came to me that morning:

Leadership And Life Lessons I Learned From My Guitar

1. Don't allow people or things to STRING you along.

2. Don't FRET over things you cannot change.

3. Each of the six STRINGS can represent a different aspect of my life or business. They can represent health, finances, my marriage, my social life, relationships, sales, marketing, production, leadership, a poor performer, results, productivity or morale. When one is out of tune, it impacts the success of my overall life or business.

4. Sometimes you have to stick your NECK out. The only way a turtle gets anywhere is by sticking their neck out. A quote by Richard Branson sums this up very well; "The risk takers may not live forever but the overly cautious do not live at all."

5. Sometimes you just have to stop everything, TUNE and start again. I do believe lessons learned in a unique way stay with us longer. These have stuck with me.

Chapter 56. Daily Task List Readjustment, Cancer, Perspective and What Matters Is Measured!

Perspective:

I've seen life from many different perspectives. Being extremely nearsighted as a kid added to this. I've seen life from having to rush to grade school to get a front row seat so I could see the blackboard. I've seen life as a line drive in Little League that just cleared the top of my glove because of this nearsightedness and the blood that ensued.

Eventually, I've seen life through glasses, contacts and cataract surgery in both eyes.

I've viewed life as a son, brother, friend, cousin, husband, father and papaw.

I've viewed life and work as an employee, co-worker, supervisor, manager, Area Manager and as a Human Resources Manager.

Every view gained a new perspective.

In 2014 - 2015, I gained an entirely new perspective I wasn't counting on; a cancer survivor.

I don't know if there is an appropriate amount of time that must pass to be a survivor, but I don't want to rush it. I want to enjoy and make each precious day as productive as possible.

My journey to being a cancer survivor has been very quick and painful.

If you have ever heard any of my leadership presentations or keynotes; you have heard me say; "what matters is measured." In these presentations, I am referring to quality, productivity, safety and attendance.

In this chapter, I am referring to you. Yes, you matter. How are you measuring your health? I shudder to think of where this would've led if I didn't have a 30+ year habit of annual physicals.

I don't want to beat around the bush; this recovery is painful as heck. I had to totally rearrange my daily task lists and goals. I didn't have control over this, but I do control my daily efforts. This occurs every day in the work place. There have been many before me with worse situations and they have made it. I have altered my days to heal as quickly as possible.

Now I want to dispel a horrible myth and lie. I've heard these words and have also said them in my life. I was wrong! *"If you don't have your health, you don't have anything."*

For a couple of months, I did not have my health. When I did not have my health, I wrote the things I DID have;

1. My Faith

2. Sandy, my wife and best friend of nearly 40 years. She has always been by my side and was a great care giver.

3. My family and friends I love and care for and that love, care and have prayed for me.

4. The benefit of great leaders and mentors in my life that have given me the ability to educate and share with others.

5. The drive to see leaders succeed in leadership and life.

So you see, even when I didn't have my health, I had plenty. If you are going through any health challenges, take a few minutes to jot down what you HAVE.

Life and leadership WILL deal you some unexpected and unscheduled interruptions. Stop focusing on these interruptions.

Focus on what you have and how you can put the life interruptions in your rear view mirror. Once you get them in the rear view mirror, push on the gas. That's the only way life interruptions get smaller. Don't set around idling. You will never "get better" without your foot on the gas.

Chapter 57. I'll Learn Your Name If You Are Still Here In Six Months!

After a keynote presentation in Arkansas, I was visiting with a manager about their group experiencing excessive turnover. We were discussing the cost to the organization and the instability caused by high turnover.

He then shared a comment that one of their training managers (a boss NOT a Leader) says to all new team members as they begin on this team; "I will not go the trouble of learning your name until you've been here six months and I know you are sticking around."

If I know you are "For Me", I will walk through doors for you. If I think you are "For Yourself" or "Against Me," I will do just enough to get by or leave. Telling me you are not willing to learn my name is a pretty good indicator you are not "For Me."

Does this give you a clue as to why their turnover is high? If this were the private sector; poor profitability and customer service caused by excessive turnover would have probably already removed this business from the poor leadership gene pool.

This was a government organization. Every taxpayer is paying for the excessive turnover caused by poor leadership. Depending on which article you read and the nature of the position, I've seen the cost of replacing and retraining from $4,000 to $20,000.

I'm not saying this is the only reason for the turnover, but ask yourself this; don't you believe the leader of the person making these comments knows about it? They may even laugh and agree with it? If they do, they are NOT a leader, they are a boss.

My suggestion to this person and to you if this exists in your organization; terminate this manager. No warning, no progressive discipline and no performance improvement plan. This is misconduct and a display of poor judgment. I'm not aware of any leadership positions where good judgment is not essential. It doesn't matter if your revenue originates from a customer making a purchase or a citizen paying taxes.

Chapter 58. What 90% Of Managers Won't Do And How That Can Affect Your Income!

When I was first promoted in 1978, my manager spent a day with me going over a how to build an Educated, Engaged and Accountable team. I am so grateful he expected more than distributing tasks and putting out fires. My life and career would have been so different.

Three things stuck out at the end of the day:

1. I would be asked, "show me what you are doing to improve your team" on a regular basis. I was expected to produce documentation.

2. Supervisors supervise, managers manage but true leaders get better. I didn't know it at the time, but the seeds for "The Power Of Better" were planted that day.

3. Do these things throughout your career, EVEN IF YOU ARE NOT REQUIRED TO and you will always be in the top 10% of managers.

How can it affect your income? If you have any type of performance based compensation plan, this should be obvious. What difference would it make in your life to be in the top 10% of income in your position vs. the top 20% for a 20-30 year career? It could be huge.

Let me give you an example; A person making $50,000 annually and receiving a three percent increase per year will make $286,764 more in twenty years than a person making $40,000 and receiving the same three percent annual increase. 1.61 million vs. 1.34 million in twenty years. Is that worth the extra effort?

You will go through your career with one of two mindsets, the Leader/Owner Mindset or the boss/employee mindset. The top 10% will have the Leader/Owner Mindset.

Many of your peers will be satisfied and will be allowed to remain on the payroll while maintaining. Why not take advantage of their choice of mediocrity for you and your family? We all have to be doing something. Why not choose to be excellent at whatever you are doing and see where that takes you.

Chapter 59. Learning From Our Mistakes.

Most of us carry smart phones. I've always known the smart phones are only as smart as the one holding the phone. In 2013, I discovered this in a very embarrassing way. I was asked to share a song and speak on leadership at the Kiwanis Club meeting in my hometown. It was a meeting honoring law enforcement, fire departments and elected officials. What a great audience for a discussion on leadership.

The meeting was scheduled for 11-19-13 and I needed to be there at 11:45AM. No problem, I put the event in my SMART phone with a two day and two hour follow-up. The only problem is my big fingers hit 11-18-13. Once it goes into the SMART phone, it is forgotten.

I showed up on 11-18-13. There were others at the location. We spoke and visited. I had my guitar, and they asked if I was sharing a song with them. I said yes, and it appeared I was at the right place. Once I got inside, they invited me to have a plate of catfish. I complied, ate and visited.

I had not seen the person that invited me; Bob, but I saw many familiar faces. It appeared someone else was also on the program. When I asked about Bob, they informed me Bob was a Kiwanis member and I was at the local Lions Club meeting.

Right place, right time, wrong date. He said their program was full, or they would allow me to share also. I gracefully thanked him but said I would prefer to draw as little attention to me as possible. I was at the wrong civic club meeting. I offered to pay for my meal and slip out, but he chose to have $10 worth of fun with me. I did enjoy the meal, meeting and program.

At the conclusion of the meeting, I immediately called Bob and explained I was a little early to the meeting. Twenty-four hours early to be exact. We had a good laugh and he asked if I wanted to share this at the correct meeting or should he. I said I would share with the group and use this as a leadership lesson.

On the correct date at the correct meeting, I shared my promptness to the group. I also shared the leadership lesson I had learned from this experience. I always try to learn from each failure.

Leadership Lesson # 1 – There are no free lunches. Even though I did not have to pay for my fish dinner, there was a cost. There will be a cost incurred every time I run into an attendee of the wrong meeting. The statute of limitations may never expire on this mistake.

Leadership Lesson # 2 – When you mess up, fess up, fix it and move on. We all make mistakes and the absolute worst thing you can do is not accept responsibility and attempt to point the finger at others. I did not even try to think I was given the wrong date or any other excuse. You can have excuses or results.

Leadership Lesson # 3 – If you can't laugh at yourself, I don't want to work with you, for you or even be around you. This would make for a very miserable day.

Everything turned out okay plus I gathered more lessons in leadership and life. Since what I do consists of mainly of real life stories, I can always use another story.

The greatest lessons I have learned in my life have been through the stories of others. Maybe this will help you "get better".

Chapter 60. Where Is A Leader When You Need One?

A few years ago, a photo made the rounds on social media. It was a photo of a group of National Guard Honor Guards from various states. It was taken in front of a flag-draped casket. It was published on social media with the caption: We put the FUN in funeral – your fearless honor guard from various states.

First, the photo and caption were sickening to me. I once witnessed a fallen hero being flown into my home town. You can read about it on my blog No, What I Saw Was Americans.

You can also listen to a song I wrote honoring veterans, fire and law enforcement at www.ForServing.com. The song asks a very tough question; "are you proud of what you've done, with what they died for?" I doubt any of the willing participants in that photo are proud of their actions.

The purpose of this chapter is not to bring additional shame to these guardsmen and women. This chapter is about the absence of leadership and the presence of poor judgment in this group.

There are 14 individuals in this photo, and I will give them the benefit of the doubt and hope they set a timer on the camera. Surely there weren't 15 individuals involved. Let's examine how this occurred.

Did it begin like this?

They were all sitting around a table that morning. They all began grinning and nodding their head. In unison, all 14 shouted "let's make a picture of all of us with a flag draped casket with a caption that we put the FUN in funeral."

NO! NO! NO! It began as all good AND bad ideas begin. It began with one person thinking this would be cute or funny. Through intimidation, authority or persuasion, they were able to convince 13 other followers this would be an acceptable thing to do.

Not one leader stepped up from the 13 and said NO! Again, being an optimist and wanting to give this group the benefit of the doubt, I'm guessing there were more in the group given an opportunity to be in the photo but declined.

This brings up lesson number one.

There are two sides to integrity; The moral side and the character side. In my seminar, I give this example; my grandson calls me, and he is so proud of himself. He says Papaw; there were some boys bullying another boy and I didn't join in. Aren't you proud of me?

The answer is yes, I am proud of him, but then I ask this question; what did you do to stop the others from bullying the boy? If the answer is nothing, he has the moral side of integrity but is lacking on the character side.

There are many good people that don't do the wrong thing, but they are also inactive in doing the right thing. They make mediocre followers, poor leaders.

Lesson Two. Years ago, a friend of mine shared the rule of the Four W's with me. I have used it many times in my decision-making process and also share it in my seminar. They are;

1. What's the best that can happen?
2. What's the worst that can happen?
3. What will likely happen? (normally something in between the best and worst)
4. Will I still be okay if the worst happens while attempting to get to the best? Am I willing to accept the impact this will have on my health, finances, marriage or relationships?

Most humans never get past number one, but the Four W's have helped me make better decisions. It allows you to take risks but does not endorse risky behavior.

Lesson Three. In my HR career, I always said, "everyone has an empty gun. It is my job to not give them a bullet to shoot at me."

This group of 14 handed out hi-capacity clips. One leader could have stepped up and saved these 14 a lot of mental anguish. Where is a leader when you need one?

I'm not going to guess at what punishment will be handed out for this use of extremely bad judgment but I'm guessing they don't have many military positions where good judgment is optional.

Chapter 61. Pick Your Battles And Never Miss A Good Opportunity To Shut Up!

I learned years ago it was very easy to win a battle while losing the war. It's like being ahead at halftime in a football game. It feels good in the locker room at halftime but is easily forgotten if you lose the game.

I want to share a few examples of self-discipline, personal growth and restraint.

The first example involves a team member that stole $32,000 from the company. He had created a very elaborate time reporting scheme that increased his paycheck immensely. His plan worked for over a year until we noticed a red flag, caught the problem and terminated the employee.

No one questioned the termination for theft, but I thought we should do more. I felt we should prosecute the ex-employee and I took my suggestion to our general attorney. He did not agree. When I asked him to "make me feel good about not prosecuting him", he stated we were a large company, this was an individual and it would make us look bad. I disagreed and asked him what else he had.

He also said it was embarrassing it took a year to discover the theft. I stated that was not an embarrassment to me because of the details and the elaborate scheme he had implemented. I suggested we prosecute. The general attorney again said no.

I asked one more question. I asked, "are you saying if I could figure a way to steal $5 million dollars, you would fire me but you wouldn't prosecute?" He said Gilbert, we are not prosecuting this person, we are through, get out of my office.

As you can tell, I'm still not satisfied with not prosecuting that person, but I had gone as far as I could in making my case and was unsuccessful. I was satisfied that any further discussion would not result in a prosecution. It would only hurt the very important working relationship between myself and the general attorney. I chose never to miss an opportunity to shut up and left his office.

My second example involved an American flag. My dad was a veteran and when he passed away my mom was given a flag at the funeral. When my mom passed away, my sister and I were sitting on the floor at my mom's house going through a box of family items. I would pull something from the box, lay it on the floor, and one of us would say they would like to have that item. It was going very smoothly but every time I reached in the box, my hand brushed against the flag I wanted oh, so badly.

I reached the point where the box was empty except for the flag. I placed the flag on the floor and as a result of personal development and growth, I said these words; Teresa, there is probably nothing I can say that would make you say, you are right, you should have the flag. There is also probably nothing you can say that would make me say, you should get the flag. How about flipping a coin to see who gets the flag? She agreed.

Now I had a very good argument prepared to get that flag but I decided not to use it. The argument was very weakly based on gender. I have yet to find a female that thought gender would be a good basis for an argument. I was even prepared to say, "dad would've wanted me to have it." I would hate to go in front of even a bad attorney with that argument.

I do believe I could've convinced my sister I should get the flag. I do believe I could've made a valid argument that would have lasted all the way to when my sisters head hit the pillow that night. I do believe she would've been angry at herself and me when she had time to lay and reflect.

The moral of the story is my relationship with my sister was much more important than the flag. I saw an opportunity for a favorable resolution for both parties, and it worked.

Oh, in case you're wondering, I got the flag. Pick your battles and never miss a good opportunity to shut up!

Chapter 62. There May Be Only One Boss Like This But They Move Around A Lot.

I believe this boss deserves her own chapter.

My favorite oldest daughter worked for a boss years ago. Understand, this was a boss, not a leader. My daughter requested a day off to attend the funeral of her father-in-law. The funeral was out of town, so a full day was necessary and requested.

This was the response of her boss;

"Amber, I will let you off, but I need you to know you are putting us in a hell of a bind by taking the day off."

Was my daughter's boss "For Her", "Against Her" or "For Herself"? Did you feel the warmth and compassion in her response?

Would you attend the funeral, come back to work and bust your rear for this boss? Or would you attend the funeral, come back to work and request a transfer to a different department? My daughter chose door number two.

This was my daughter's first introduction to a total lack of leadership and this type of boss, not leader. If you remain in the business world, you will encounter these people.

I assured my daughter one good thing would occur as a result of this. I would share this with thousands of people, and I have. I know that bosses' evil twin has been in many of my sessions. Maybe they will change. If I can prevent one person from feeling like my daughter felt that day, I've had a good session.

Chapter 63. The Layoff Prevention Plan

Years ago, the daughter of a friend of mine was graduating and entering the workforce. She asked her dad how to never be laid off.

My friend and I had a good laugh about the word never. I told my friend I didn't have a Layoff Elimination Plan, but I did have a Layoff Prevention Plan. It only had three steps.

1. Do your job to the best of your ability. This means every aspect of quality, productivity, safety and attendance.

2. Constantly seek guidance from leadership on how you can get better. Always strive to close the gap between your performance and your potential. Don't compare your beginning with the middle of someone else.

3. Do this with a great attitude.

These three items are the best advice I can give anyone at any level or tenure. Shortcut one of the steps and you've just made yourself much less valuable to the organization.

Chapter 64. I'm Going To Tell You Something But

"I'm going to tell you something, but you can't tell where you heard it and if you say I told you; I'll call you a liar."

How many of us have heard this statement? How many of us have said those words before we knew better?

As you think of those words, I would like for you to imagine fireworks, a big red flag waving from side to side and a marching band led by two majorettes carrying a huge banner. On the banner in huge letters is the word "GOSSIP".

Are you ready to be a contributor to cancer in your organization? I hope not.

If you are a leader, do not allow anyone to put this monkey on your back. It has diarrhea. If you agree to accept this monkey with your vow of secrecy, you have just accepted the equivalent of a kickback from the mob. You have sold your soul for a small, juicy tidbit of gossip.

You are now labeled as one that is willing to receive gossip. Right or wrong, it will be assumed you will also be willing to share gossip.

Also, if you are in a position of leadership, if the situation implodes, you will be thrown under the bus with absolutely no hesitation. You had knowledge and did absolutely nothing.

I developed a canned statement that kept most of these monkeys off my back. Whenever I heard the words, "I'm going to tell you something but", I stopped them before they continued.

This is my canned statement; "Before you proceed, I need to let you know something. If you share something with me that makes me aware of a policy violation or something that increases the liability of our company; I will address the situation. Knowing that, what did you want to share?"

Many would say, never mind and head for the door. These were managers so before they left, I completed my canned statement.

"You also have the responsibility to protect this company. If you are aware of a situation, let's discuss it and see if we can come up with a solution."

Some stayed; some said never mind, and left.

Gossip is cancer in your organization. It can undermine morale and trust as discretely as a thief in the night.

Dave Ramsey's organization in Nashville, Tennessee has the best policy and description of gossip I've ever heard.

You get one strike. The next occurrence of gossip leads to dismissal. You know the rules and consequences up front.

I also love their definition of gossip. Gossip is anything negative about a person, department or the company that is shared with someone that cannot correct the problem. Negatives only go up. Positives go down. Negatives do not go laterally.

Gossip is an individual and organizational culture established over time but can be corrected immediately. It is corrected with humility, acceptance it has existed, a line drawn in the sand and a consequence.

Chapter 65. We Will Always Beat Me.

Early in my career, I was an enabler. If you had a problem, all you had to do was bring it to my office and I would take it. It was like I had a sign outside my office and was wearing a tee shirt that said "bring me your problems." Eventually, I began to feel like a porta potty at a music festival; the recipient of what others did not want.

Something had to change. Bob's Rule from 1980 resurfaced; "If I have to do your job, I don't need you." I began a new process. This was probably a suggestion of a mentor, leader, seminar or book. I would hate to go through life totally dependent on my original thoughts.

When someone shared a problem, I acknowledged the problem and requested they bring me two possible solutions. This opened the floodgates of ideas. Many were so much better than mine. Our creativity is amazing when challenged.

This drastically reduced my work load and stress level. This is a form of delegation and must be mastered to be successful at a higher level.

However, to reap the full benefit of this process, you must possess one trait. You must be willing to truthfully, honestly consider the ideas of others as sometimes better than yours. This process does not mix well with a large ego.

Chapter 66. Feedback! Always Sought, Seldom Found!

A few years ago, I had a great Thanksgiving as usual with football, food, deer hunting, food, family, fellowship and more food. We also had a fire in the fire pit on a couple of days. My youngest grandson, Kasen, was placed in charge of the fire pit after the fire was started.

His job was to keep the fire just right, not too high or too low. Later, the fire was surrounded by many family members as S'mores were prepared. Kasen never forgot his responsibility. It burned steadily for over 10 hours until bedtime.

The next morning Kasen and I went deer hunting. I told him how everyone had commented on how great the fire was. I wish I could share with you the look I received. It was a big grin of humility, pride and "ah shucks" without saying a word and a small head nod. When he looked away, the grin remained.

I've seen this same grin when he is praised for a job well done in baseball or football.

My oldest grandson, Kel is a great swimmer. He has won some awards, a high school swim scholarship and shaved time off his previous best many times. Whether it's being there screaming and rooting him on or a congratulatory phone call, I can't imagine not praising him and getting "the grin."

Man, I love being a papaw.

In my keynotes and seminars, I discuss feedback at length. It is called engagement and with technology it is becoming a lost art.

I have anonymously surveyed over 200 managers with two questions:

1. Do you believe your immediate supervisor is "For You", "Against You" or "For Themselves?

2. Outside of an annual appraisal, how long has it been since your immediate supervisor has discussed expectations, progress, praise, the company's vision or culture?

Over 65% felt their immediate supervisor was "Against them" or "For Themselves."

Over 70% said outside of their annual appraisal; there was never any discussion about expectations, progress, praise, the company's vision or culture. My favorite answer was; "I don't remember when this discussion took place, but I know my hair was a different color."

This is the greatest cause of poor morale in organizations.

It has been said the last applause most people receive is at their high school graduation. There are only 17 vertebrae between a kick in the rear and a pat on the back.

I highly recommend applause and a pat on the back. Instead of the grin I received, you may receive higher productivity, better morale and reduced turnover.

Chapter 67. Papaw, When Will Spider-Man Stop Growing?

When will spider man stop growing? This was a question my youngest grandson, Kasen, asked about a spider man we put in a glass of water. This spider man was very tiny when we placed it in the glass and eventually absorbed enough water that it grew to fit the size of the glass.

Later that night after a Walker, Texas Ranger and he was asleep, my other grandson, Kel and I sat at the counter with a glass of milk, bowl of cereal and spider-man. I thought about what spider-man and I had in common. As usual, both of my grandsons prompt so many of my thoughts. As adults, we need to ask who, what when and why more often.

From the time we begin learning, until we leave this planet; we absorb what is around us and either grow or decline. We grow physically, mentally, financially and spiritually in our careers and relationships by what we absorb.

Imagine this empty glass with us inside. Pour in some "what we read", "what we listen to", "what we watch", "what we attend" and some "who we hang around". Top this off with a large dose of "what are you going to do with it" and depending on the quality of the ingredients, it could be a formula for success.

Each ingredient plays a huge part of who we are and what we do. We absorb from each of these to form or change us. If one or more of these ingredients are not present in your life, the others fill in for them.

Many only have the "who we hang around" ingredient in their life because they never read, listen to, watch or attend anything that helps them grow. This severely restricts your knowledge level. This is not because of lack of intelligence; it is because the lack of exposure to different ingredients. Since wisdom is the application of knowledge, you have restricted your opportunities for wisdom.

So to answer the question, spider man is probably as large as he can get because of his limitations. His main limitation is the size of the glass. As humans, we choose our limitations. We are not in a glass.

Kel and Kasen, I want to thank you so much for reminding me most of my limitations are truly self-imposed. Most of the time, it just boils down to a lack of good ingredients.

Warning; severe shrinkage occurs when spider man is pulled from the "growth ingredient" which is water. The same occurs to us when we are away from "growth ingredients" such as educational opportunities. He or we will NOT remain the same!

Chapter 68. The Life Saving Value Of Education.

Have you ever had to do something you did not want to do? We all have. Years ago, I had to take CPR. I thought it was a waste of my time. I thought there were many things I could be doing more productive. The CPR dummy was bald like me, and I asked for a wig. Even after all of my whining, moaning and complaining, I still had to take CPR. Later on, I re-certified and still complained.

The frustration of taking CPR had long passed. I was certain it was a skill set I would never use. That changed suddenly in our home in Fayetteville, Arkansas in January of 1986. I was in my den visiting with someone when they had a heart attack. I had to pull him out of a recliner, place him on the floor and performed CPR for eight to ten minutes until the ambulance arrived.

Later that afternoon, the doctor said I saved his life by performing CPR. I had broken a rib, but he said that was very common because of the adrenaline flowing.

This is a good news, bad news, phenomenal news and phenomenal, phenomenal news story. The good news is I had the training and skills to save someone's life. The bad news is the person passed away five months later as a result of a blood clot going to their heart. The phenomenal news is this person accepted their faith in that five-month period. The phenomenal, phenomenal news is this person was my Dad.

I don't complain anymore about having to learn anything new. The moral of the story is you never know how what you learn could help you or someone else.

I'm a firm believer if we don't read it, listen to it, watch it, attend it or hang around it; we will never get it. If we don't get it, we can't share it. It is impossible to get better without increasing your education.

Chapter 69. You May Only Get One Opportunity To Say Or Do The Right Thing!

Years ago, my wife took a picture of our two grandsons fishing on Lake Palestine in Texas. The moment she captured will never occur again. The sun setting, the shadows, the time of day; everything was perfect.

Leadership and life are much like the timing of that photo. Many times we will have only one perfect opportunity to do or say the right thing. There is no cut, copy, paste in leadership and life; only new opportunities. There is no rewind. We must be prepared. How do we prepare ourselves?

Many people say "experience is the best teacher." I have probably said this many times in my life and now realize how wrong I was. Experience is the most costly, painful and time-consuming teacher available. Experience is only the best teacher when it is someone else's experience.

I now prefer Education. When I was hired as a telephone repairman, I'm so thankful they didn't hand me a pair of climbers and tell me to go climb poles and get experience.

What about the doctor that does your surgery? Would you like them to practice on you for their experience or be educated?

What if a person has to perform CPR on you? It's an easy choice when it impacts you, isn't it? Education OR Experience? Personally I prefer both. Education AND Experience.

What about when it impacts others? It is still better to rely on education than wait on experience. We've all heard the cliché "you only get one opportunity to make a first impression." Big whoopee. You only get one chance at each second and third impression also. Get it right.

Every interaction with others is associated with either pain or pleasure. What are we doing to improve those impressions and interactions? I suggest education.

In my management development sessions, I share some of the lessons I've learned through personal and mentor's experience. Many of the lessons I've learned in management and Human Resources would've been much less painful, costly and time consuming if learned through education rather than experience.

I'm shocked at the percent of adults that never read a non-fiction book after high school. I'm a firm believer if I don't read it, attend it, listen to it, watch it or hang around it; I won't get it. If I don't get it, I can't share it.

I missed a question when I was twenty-four years old that still makes me feel like an idiot. I was at my first external leadership seminar in Little Rock at the Camelot Hotel. The instructor asked this question; when does your education end? I thought it was a trick question.

I remember flipping open my brand new folio with my name and the Bell emblem on the bottom right (as I type this, I can still smell that new leather). I remember writing with my brand new chrome Cross pen; "When your education ends depends on whether you are pursuing a high school education, Associate, Bachelor, Masters or Doctorate Degree."

I knew I had every base covered. Pick me! Pick me! I am so glad he did NOT pick me. Imagine my embarrassment when he picked someone else and they gave the one-word answer of "NEVER". If we ever want to "get better", our education never ends.

Today I use books (mostly E-books), podcasts, blogs, webinars and seminars to increase my opportunities for doing and saying the right things. All of these help me to appreciate "The Power Of Better".

Chapter 70. Life Will Give You TMO's (Teaching Moment Opportunities). Don't Blow Them!

Early in my Human Resources career, there was a change in company policy that created over 500 grievances. They all came through my office for handling. I remember all 500+ being stacked on my desk.

One day a newly promoted manager came to my office to discuss an issue. He asked if he could shut the door and looked very nervous. He finally settled into a chair in front of my desk.

He had just taken over a new crew, and there was a practice allowed for years that was costing the company money and was hurting customer service. He wanted to stop the practice but it could result in ...."a grievance." His voice dropped to a whisper as he said the words "a grievance."

I could see the fear in his eyes. I am so thankful he was tall. That made it much easier to see him over the 500+ grievances stacked between us. It was so tempting to laugh at his concern over one grievance, but this was huge to him. I knew this was a teaching moment opportunity.

I never mentioned my grievances. I gave suggestions for drawing a line in the sand and changing the policy. If it hurt profitability or customer service and was not a bargained for privilege, I agreed it should be changed.

We discussed how to go about the change and if it resulted in a grievance, it would be handled. I then gave a piece of advice from a mentor in my career. Never let the fear of a grievance keep you from doing the right thing. That was a teaching moment opportunity, and I'm so thankful I handled it the way I did.

I recently read an article about a high school football game in Texas where the score was 91-0 in favor of Aledo over Fort Worth Western Hills. One of the parents of the losing team filed a formal complaint against the winning coach for "bullying". That's a much abused buzz word these days. The complaint was investigated and they found no grounds to support the bullying complaint.

Wow! This parent missed a great teaching moment opportunity about competition and life. The actions of that parent filing that complaint will have a much more adverse long-term impact on their child than the butt-whipping on the football field.

The parent missed the first opportunity at a teaching moment. The parent then had a second opportunity for a teaching moment in humility unless they were too prideful. They should have withdrawn the complaint and apologized to their son and the coach.
In a football game, referees are there to insure fair play. The winners are determined by skill, talent and preparation. Leadership and life are the same.

Life, health, finances, marriages and careers do NOT hand out Participation Trophies. The trophies are for winning! Fair is a place where they have merry-go-rounds and Ferris wheels. We all need to learn that at an early age.

Twenty Thanksgivings from now, if this parent does the right thing, they will laugh about the butt-whipping on the football field. If the parent is too prideful and fails to admit a mistake; they will NEVER laugh about the complaint. The best teaching moment opportunity for that parent is "Crow is best eaten when warm, not cold and crusty."

Be aware when life deals you teaching moment opportunities. You may only get one chance to get it right and help someone else "get better".

Chapter 71. Losing Your Barbara Will Cost You Thousands!

I mentioned earlier in the book some companies drop the ball on Engaging with their team members. This is one of those stories. Hopefully, you will see the cause, cost and consequences of not engaging with team members.

Barbara was just one of those employees. She did a great job. She strived for improvement. She got along great with others. She loved her company and she had a great attitude. She was the total employee package.

What makes Barbara even more exceptional was she was laid off due to low seniority, hired back a few years later and still kept this high work ethic and great attitude. In fact, this was recognized and Barbara was promoted into management.

Sadly, later in her career, the love of the company and her attitude wavered, but never disappeared. Why did it waver? Poor leadership with a total lack of Engagement thrown in.

A few years ago I called Barbara to see how everything was going. One of the red flags I heard was the company was not like it used to be, but she still enjoyed her career.

I asked Barbara two questions. First; was her immediate supervisor "For Her," "Against Her" or " For Themselves? " The second question was "outside of an annual review, how long had it been since her immediate supervisor sat down one-on-one and discussed expectations and progress?"

Barbara's answered the second question first which answered the first question. Barbara stated even though her immediate supervisor was down the hall, they had not even spoken in months. That statement also answered the first question.

When a supervisor has zero Engagement with a team member, they do not default to they are "For Me." This lack of Engagement continued for another year or two. Barbara became retirement eligible, and when given the opportunity, she retired. She told me she had no idea if she was valued as a team member or if she made any contribution to the organization.

I know there was a huge training curve to get a replacement up to the level of Barbara's expertise. It probably cost the organization tens of thousands of dollars.

One hundred percent of that cost could have been eliminated or at least deferred. How? By the simple act of talking. That's right. If Barbara's supervisor had carved out just a few minutes a month to communicate and Engage with Barbara, she would have stayed.

If you are a Manager or Supervisor, engaging with your team members is a basic part of your job. When you get better at Engagement, your team will get better.

Chapter 72. Worms And Good Team Members Don't Like Toxic Environments.

A few years ago, one of my neighbors decided to disc one of his hay fields. Discing is normally used to get rid of ruts and rough ground. After discing, a field is much smoother. Many times, a farmer will use a breaking plow prior to discing. This gets much deeper into the soil and prepares the land for discing.

One day I was driving by while my neighbor was using the breaking plow. I decided now would be a great time to take a break and go pond fishing. I knew there would be acres of freshly turned soil, and I figured my favorite bait, which is worms, would be plentiful. I pulled in the pasture.

I walked through the pasture with a coffee can in pure anticipation of the big bream or crappie that would fall prey to my first cast. It was late in the day. I could envision closing the day with my wife and I watching the sun set in lawn chairs. I would have a fishing pole in my hand and she would have her Smart phone in hers. In fact, I remember pulling in and thinking if the worms were plentiful enough, it could be the beginning of my own worm farm. My grandsons and I would never have to purchase a container of worms. Never, ever.

No worms were found. Had they heard I was coming? I went back to my truck and pulled closer to the tractor and plow. In fact, I began walking right behind the tractor. This would allow me to catch the dirt just as it was turned. Worms should be scurrying to dig back in. My can should be full in no time.

Still no worms. With all that freshly turned dirt, not one worm. The fish were safe another day. I waved at my neighbor and drove off. The break was over, and I began looking for my next project.

Initially, I couldn't understand the absence of worms. Then it hit me. You see, over the years, this hay field had been sprayed many times for weeds. It had also been fertilized many times with commercial fertilizers.

Through the years, this piece of land had gradually become toxic territory. The worms had moved on. They didn't have to stay in a toxic environment. They found better dirt.

Many companies and organizations have toxic environments. They allow bosses (not leaders) to remain employed that still believe yelling, screaming, intimidation and demeaning others is an acceptable or effective form of leadership.

Their bosses don't have either the knowledge, skills or guts to address this, so the toxic environment continues. The business equivalent of toxic chemicals is dumped on team members. Many will leave. Many will lose all respect for management and shift into the mode that cost companies billions of dollars each year. It is the mode of doing just enough to get by.

Toxic work environments also exist where there is a lack of Education, Engagement or Accountability. The absence of any of these creates a workforce that will never get close to their potential.

Organizations must get better in eliminating toxic work environments. They are very easy to recognize. All you normally have to do is look at results, turnover and morale. In some cases, turnover may be low because of a lack of other opportunities. In these cases, results and morale will identify your toxic territory. Once a toxic environment is identified, all you have to do is train, develop or in some cases, eliminate the cause of the toxicity.

I have two wonderful daughters. They have always been my rule of thumb on work environments. I ask myself "would I want my daughters working in this environment?" If the answer is No, I then ask what it would take to change the answer to Yes. Then it is time to go to work in making the environment better. Making things better is just a natural habit of true leaders.

Chapter 73. It Will Be A Long Uphill Battle If Fun Is Not Included!

Do you work around fun people? Are you a fun person? There are so many organizations with horrible morale. One of the main reasons is no one likes to have fun at work. Many times in leadership, we get so caught up in the day-to-day pressures, we eventually forget how to have fun.

In my 12 years as the primary human resources contact to 2200 team members, I lost my hair but kept my sense of humor. I am thankful it worked out that way because I would sure hate to have a full head of hair with no sense of humor.

Many times, upper-level management fall into the no fun trap. It sure changes morale when team members can see upper-level management let their guard down and have fun. I'm not talking silly fun; I'm talking good clean fun normally delegated to somebody else.

I will give you a couple of examples of Mary and Mike. Both were president of our division at different times. I've seen Mary sing and dance on stage with her direct reports to a parody of the song "Proud Mary".

I've seen Mike dress up as Diana Ross and pantomime "Stop In The Name Of Love" after the marketing group met a very challenging sales goal. I hate to mention that because it reminds me how ugly Mike was as a woman. I may have to poke my mind's eye out again to clear that memory.

Both Mike and Mary liked to have fun, but they held their teams fully accountable. We had very challenging goals but were able to have fun and celebrate if successful.

My point is you can be a successful leader AND have fun. It is not a choice of being a successful leader OR having fun. Plus, time does pass more quickly when you're having fun and getting better.

Chapter 74. Are You Closing Your Gap?

As a farm kid, I heard "be sure and close the gap" many times.
As an adult, I have worked feverishly to close the gap between who I am and who I can become.

I recently gave a short presentation at an entertainment night during the Mid-Winter Lions Conference. Their theme for the conference was "Strengthening Pride Through Innovation and Technology." Innovation MUST have an origin.

If something is not read, watched, listened to or attended to originate the thought process, you will be just like the line from that George Jones song, "I'm still the same ol' me."

"I'm still the same ol' me" is a song lyric from a country song. It should not be your mission statement. One of the most rewarding benefits of "getting better" is closing the performance – potential gap?

This is only accomplished by reading, listening, watching, attending and most importantly, implementing. This will put you in that Top 10%.

Chapter 75. Tale Of Two Pities

Here is the first Pity. I pity supervisors placed in leadership positions and not provided the Education, Engagement and held Accountable for producing results. These newly promoted supervisors do not have a fair start.

The next Pity is based on a true story.

On a Thursday, a sixteen-year employee finishes loading a truck with a forklift. He pulls the forklift by the office while completing his paperwork on loading the truck. The Plant Manager walks in and asks the employee if he was aware he left the forklift running. He didn't remember leaving it running but didn't argue.

The next day the employee is required by his immediate supervisor to write an incident report about leaving the forklift running. He is advised it is considered a critical safety infraction. He complies and is sent home while the company considers further action.

On Monday, he is called in, advised his write up does not reflect sincerity or remorse and is terminated. There was no progressive discipline in the past or history of ignoring safety practices.

Before I go any farther I want to make this clear; I know the importance of safety and consider ANY safety infraction critical BUT I also know the difference in a performance problem and a mistake. I also handle them totally differently.

Here is my second pity. I pity the supervisor, HR Manager and Plant Manager with this feather in their cap or line item on their resume. Could they terminate this employee? You bet, but that is not the correct question. The correct question is "is termination the right thing to do?"

Another question is "am I terminating this employee for what they have done or for what I haven't done?" Another question is "what leadership tools have I used to correct the problem?" If I were involved in this dismissal, I would hate to answer an attorney on the "Seven Tests Of Just Cause." Maybe their company just uses the "One Test Of Just Cause."

If the words "make an example out of him" were ever used in these termination discussions, I pity
their leadership hierarchy even more.

If they wanted to "send a message" to other employees, they did. The message is "if you work here, you don't matter."

In my opinion, this Tale Of Two Pities shows the extreme of doing too little and doing too much. They reflect under reacting and overreacting, in my opinion.

You may disagree, but I believe I could have "Led Like I Own It", used the "Leadership Toolkit", corrected the problem, and had a more favorable outcome on the second pity.

Chapter 76. Danger! Selfish Or Selfless Choice Ahead!

I recently saw a strong statement about selfish choices on social media and a flood of thoughts hit me.

I learned years ago in HR and through coaching myself and others, our words and actions fall into two categories; selfish or selfless.

Selfish words and actions have a foundation of anger, pride, ego and emotions. They provide temporary satisfaction to only one person as they are normally a result of zero input from others.

Selfless words and actions have a foundation of logic, reasoning and a long-term view. They consider the long term impact on many instead of one.

Most selfish words and actions could be eliminated by asking a Non "Yes Person" these words; "what do you think about _____?" The value of a Non "Yes Person" in our life is immeasurable. Most of us have access to one, but they become invisible when we enter "The Selfish Zone."

I had six different leaders in my 12 years as Area Manager – Human Resources. Each one shared their version of this statement with me in the first few weeks; "I do not need a Yes Person in your position. I need you to tell me what I need to hear, not what you think I want to hear." I need you to be an honest sounding board.

Don't be a "Yes Person." Establish who the Non "Yes People" are in your life. If you have two people that think, act and do the same; you don't need one of them.

Chapter 77. Are You A Settler?

One hundred and fifty years ago, families had dreams, goals and destinations. They packed everything they owned in a Conestoga wagon, hooked it to a team of horses, mules or oxen. They left everything comfortable behind. They left friends and family because they had a dream, goal and destination.

Invariably, something would go wrong. A horse, mule or oxen would die. A wheel would fall off, or an axle would break. Some would do whatever it took to get back on the trail to their dream, goal or destination. Many more, however, would look around and say, this doesn't look bad, I think I will settle here.

Have you settled? This occurs in different aspects at different times in all our lives. It occurs in our finances, our health, our relationships and our jobs or career. I challenge you to look in the mirror in all aspects of your life and answer the question, have I settled?

In fact, to take more ownership of this question, get a blank sheet of paper. Across the top, write the words "Have I Settled?" Down the left-hand side of the page, write my finances, my health, my friendships, my marriage and my livelihood. This is a simple exercise. Beside each aspect of your life, answer the question "Have I Settled?" A simple Yes or No will do.

This is where most books would go into a chapter on goal setting, but this is not most books. There are hundreds of books on goal setting, and you can take your pick. I have heard two descriptions of not setting goals in your life;

1. Having no written goals is like playing basketball with a backboard but no goal. There's no way to keep score. Can you imagine how foolish you would look shooting a basketball at an empty backboard?

2. Having no written goals is like bowling without lights in a bowling alley. You hear a lot of noises, but you have no idea of the score.

I have also always heard those without goals always work for those with goals. It is impossible to lead like you own it without a set of written goals. You choose.

Chapter 78. Slow Down. You're Making Me Look Bad.

What excites me more than anything when my wife and I go to the show is when I hear the movie is based on a true story. Well, this, like all the stories in this book, is based on a true story. Years ago, I had a friend accept an engineering position. He had no previous engineering experience, so he had to start from scratch and learn everything about the position.

My friend is sharp and a quick study. He picked it up quickly. After approximately a year in the position, one of the other engineers pulled him aside. He informed my friend he didn't have to be that productive to work in that department. He suggested my friend slow down a little because he was making him and the others look bad.

Now these are individuals in leadership and management positions. Here is the absolute shame of the situation. The individual that asked my friend to slow down, worked in that department over 30 years. Evidently, standards were so low or non-existent; or there was such a total lack of accountability, this department allowed this slug to continue drawing a paycheck until retirement.

What would you do if a coworker requested you slow down? Would you slow down? Would you continue as you were doing before? Would you report the individual to your manager? You can learn a lot about your own character in your answers to these questions. It is impossible to lead like you own it without character.

Chapter 79. You Are A Professional. Be Proud Of It!

Two years ago, I was asked to speak at a leadership event. I was informed I must discuss topics that pertained to the professional manager and supervisor. To be honest, at that time, when I thought of a professional, I thought of a doctor, attorney or athlete.

I've never really thought of myself as a professional when I was a manager or supervisor. Looking up the definition of professional changed my mind. A professional is defined as one engaged in a specified activity as one's main paid occupation rather than as a pastime. Most of us are not reporting to work every day as a pastime.

So here is some good news. If your main paid occupation is a manager, supervisor or HR manager; congratulations you are a professional. In fact, everyone you work with, management and non-management are all professionals. Now be proud of it and go act like a professional. Professionals get better.

Think of it this way, there are two choices, professional or amateur. If I had T-shirts available with "I Am An Amateur Manager" on the front, how many would you order? I'm betting zero.

Chapter 80. Why? It's Not Your Money.

A friend and I were recently talking leadership, and he shared a story from his organization. He is a manager, and they had overtime scheduled to complete a project prior to the deadline. They finished the project that required the overtime and reached a stopping point. Since they were on overtime, my friend suggested they wrap it up and go home.

One of the team members asked why they couldn't continue to work? He said "after all, it's not your money." My friend gave the correct answer that he treated it like his money and they should also.

What are your thoughts on this question? If a team member makes a statement implying it's not the managers money; how responsible would they be with company resources when the manager is not around?

Would you want this type of mindset in your organization? Would you allow this type of mindset in your organization? What's more important, do you have this type of mindset? Do you treat company resources like your own? Do you treat them like you own the business?

You may not view it this way, but stealing time from an organization is no different than stealing materials, tools or gas from a company vehicle. The questions in this chapter are similar to those in the chapter titled, "Slow Down, You're Making Me Look Bad."

You can learn a lot about your character by how you view statements like this.

Chapter 81. Who Owns Your Company?

One year when my youngest daughter, Autumn, was in the seventh grade, there was a "bring your daughter to work day". At the time, I was Area Manager of Human Resources in Little Rock, Arkansas. I remember her and I getting on the elevator for the nine-floor ride. There were also some of my buddies on the elevator. I introduced my daughter.

As soon as the door closed, Autumn asked who owned Southwestern Bell? I could barely concentrate with all the chatter from my buddies chiming in, "yeah, Gilbert, who owns this thing?" I explained to Autumn we were a publicly held company. I knew the next question would follow, but I hoped it would wait until we didn't have the echo boys on board. It didn't wait. She immediately asked, "what is a publicly held company?" The echo boys chimed in, "yeah, Gilbert, what is one of those things?

I said I would explain when we arrived at my office. This was a delay tactic and a method of allowing me time to figure how to explain a publicly held company to a seventh grader. I ignored the chatter from the echo boys.

When we arrived at my office, I introduced Autumn to everyone in the office. This allowed more time to prepare an answer. Finally, it was time. I had to explain a publicly held company to a seventh grader. Autumn was familiar with checking accounts, so this was my explanation; Southwestern Bell is a publicly held company. It is like a huge joint checking account with three main contributors; the customer, the employees and the shareholders. Each of the three contributes to our checking account.

The customer chooses to buy services from us. When they do, they put money in our account. We need them. We must keep them happy, or they would leave. They would take their money from our account and give it to our competitors.

The employees deposit their skills and knowledge in our account. We need them to provide services to our customers, so we have to keep them happy. We didn't want to lose their experience and expertise.

What made it a publicly held company, were our shareholders. They loaned us money by buying stock in our company. This went into our joint checking account with our customer's money and our employee's experience. We had to keep the shareholders happy by providing a good rate of return on their money or they would take their money from our account by selling their stock.

I compared keeping all three happy to juggling three bowling pins. She said she understood and we were off to the remainder of the day. I'm sure this was one of many questions of the day.

The more I thought about that off the cuff answer crafted for a seventh grader, it also made good sense to me. I've witnessed many heads nodding when telling that story in programs. If you are not a publicly held company; just use the customers and employees.

Since the title of this book is "The Power Of Better"; I hope you realize preserving the status quo, is not the best way to keep these parties happy. You must get better.

Chapter 82. There Are No "Just A" Positions Here

I believe every employee is important to a company. Every employee at every level in management and non-management are important to a company. No one is more or less important to the success of the organization.

One of my pet peeves were managers referring to someone as "just a" secretary, "just a" clerk or "just a" technician. I didn't care what level said these words; I corrected them. Our employees were more than employees. They were parents, grandparents, city board members, school board members, volunteer firemen, and I was aware of a mayor or two. They held many roles in life. Our company may be what they did for a living, but it did not define who they were.

Unless you are the Chairman or CEO, there's always a higher level. My point was every employee is important and needed, or we would not be issuing a paycheck every other week. I've seen hundreds of jobs filled and have never seen the words "just a" on any requisition. One way to get better is to eliminate the words "just a" from preceding any of your job titles.

Chapter 83. I Can Resist Everything But Temptation. - RIP - Ken Langston

I lost a good friend, Ken Langston to cancer in 2014. In March, he was okay. In August, he was gone. Ken was the husband of one of my HR buddies from Austin, TX. In 2001, Ken was one of the "Six Pack Of Fools". That was my nickname for the three couples that rode our Harleys over 3000 miles in two weeks to Daytona Bike Week and on to Key West, Florida. One of Ken's favorite sayings was; "I can resist everything but temptation."

Temptation is the test of our discipline. John Maxwell says; "Everything rises and falls on leadership." That could easily be changed to; Everything rises and falls on discipline." For most of us, knowing what to do is seldom the problem. Doing it is the problem. We are all faced with the temptation of not doing the right thing.

In fact, temptation is seldom associated with doing anything good for our business or health.

In this book, I have mapped out "becoming brilliant in the basics" through Education, Engagement and Accountability

I'm asking you to resist the temptation to do or not do anything that hurts the sustainability of your organization. Livelihoods are dependent on your sustainability.

I'm asking you to resist the temptation to ignore poor performers.

I'm asking you to resist the temptation to ignore using the leadership toolbox. This contains performance improvement plans, different levels of discipline, feedback, praise and sometimes terminations.

I'm asking you to resist the temptation to yell, scream, demean and intimidate others.

I associate temptation with shortcuts. Shortcuts are seldom successful in Leadership or Life.

If you and I could resist these temptations and if he was still here; I do believe my buddy Ken would crack a big grin as he watched us resist a big dose of temptation.

Chapter 84. Be A William.

I was about twenty minutes into a four-hour leadership program when the name first came up. One of the attendees said, "that's what William said." I just acknowledged his comment and proceeded with the program. After another thirty minutes or so, someone said, "that's what William would have done." Again, I acknowledged the comment and proceeded.

I felt pretty confident I was on the right track since it seemed someone named William agreed with many of my leadership lessons. I began to keep a stroke sheet every time someone mentioned the name William. At the end of four hours, I had five strokes on my sheet.

I had a good idea of who William was but at the end of my program, I asked; who in the world is William? I was told he was the highest level at that location for many years. He had retired a few years earlier. I was shocked that even after being gone a few years, his name was very familiar.

I asked these questions;

1. Evidently, William had a big impact here? Every head nodded.

2. Evidently, William was well thought of here? Every head nodded.

3. Evidently, William left a huge legacy here? Every head nodded.

It set me up perfectly to ask the following question; what will they say about you? Not when you are gone, what are they saying now?

Everything we do and say is building or tearing down our reputation and legacy. Everything good that is said or done builds our reputation and legacy. It is like putting another brick on a strong wall.

Every time we do or say something that hurts our reputation or legacy, it removes a brick from the wall. These bricks do not come from the top; they come from the foundation. A strong foundation is weakened quickly by the removal of just a few bricks.

We must keep adding, not removing these bricks. Personal growth and Betterment will add to your reputation and legacy. Be a William.

The Final chapter. The True Power Of Better!

Thank you for joining me on this "journey through my journals".

The job of any good writer or speaker is not telling you what to do. The job of any good writer or speaker is to share a story in a manner that encourages you to make a change.

The job of a writer or speaker is to inspire these two questions;

1. Why am I doing this?
2. Why am I not doing that?

I know some of the lessons in this book can change lives and careers. I know; they changed mine.

I cannot overemphasize the importance of building a good leadership foundation. If your leadership foundation is cracked, flawed or non-existent, it is never too late to start over or improve what you have.

The strongest foundations are built on piers. The strongest piers I've found in Leadership and Life are Education, Engagement and Accountability. None of the three can be shortened or eliminated.

My hope is as a leader, you recognize, appreciate and fully grasp the potential you have to positively influence the lives of others.

Most employees are good, honest, hard-working people that want to be challenged. They want to excel.

When I was a kid, I had a go-kart. I covered many miles on that go-kart, but I had one problem with it. It had a governor on the throttle. It limited my speed. I was unable to get the maximum performance from my motor due to this governor. Looking back, this was probably a good thing at my age.

In some cases, a lack of leadership acts as a governor on a team. You are unable to achieve maximum performance due to a lack of leadership. Don't be a governor. Turn them loose.

It all begins with a decision. It begins with the decision to intentionally get better in different aspects of Leadership and Life.

I've heard people say "well, things are better." Things don't get better.

Productivity, quality, safety, attendance, morale, profitability, finances, health and marriages do not get better until people get better.

I want you to experience the inspiration, encouragement, joy, hope and personal satisfaction that always accompany getting better.

One of the greatest benefits of personal improvement, or Betterment as call it, will be the positive ripple effect on countless others.

When you have a positive impact on others, you are changing their lives and your legacy.

That, my friend, is the true Power Of Better.

Epilogue

I've written this book to inspire every level of leadership to take an honest inventory of what they are currently doing to grow and develop their team.

Leading others is a huge responsibility. You probably have a multiple six or seven figure annual payroll. A good mindset is to consider yourself a steward of that money. Adopt a Leader/Owner Mindset.

Although this book is written for every level of leadership, most of this is written with the first two levels of leadership in mind. I have written a book I would've read and learned from in different levels and positions in my career.

A word of caution. If you think this book is not for you or beneath your skill level; you are part of the problem, not part of the solution.

How do I know this? Your first and second level leadership team told me. They continue to tell me at the conclusion of most presentations.

I've shared this information in programs with thousands of leaders. I can't count the times I've heard this statement; "This will help me immensely in my job but why is upper-level management not in here getting this message? We all need to be on this page."

This message is timeless. Getting better will never be considered "old school".

If you are not getting better and have been at your position for ten years, you don't have ten years of experience. You have one year of experience; ten times or possibly two years of experience; five times.

If you are applying for employment with me, your previous tenure means much less than what improved as a result of your actions during your tenure.

Another word of caution. In many decades of leadership, Human Resources and Leadership Coaching, I have witnessed the consequences of the intentional decision to "stay the same".

The intentional decision to "stay the same" leads to Significant Emotional Events.

On the job; these are commonly referred to as layoffs, business closures, cutbacks in benefits, no raises, missed promotions and terminations.

Off the job; these Significant Emotional Events are separations, divorces, financial crisis, estranged relationships and health issues. All of these are tracked back to a deficiency in Betterment.

One final word of caution. Be very careful in using the phrase "I already knew that." I always view that phrase as a personal invitation to look at your waistline, finances, marriage, profitability, customer service, turnover or morale to see what you are doing with what you know.

My hope is this book will lead you down the road to "getting better" in different aspects of Leadership and Life.

My hope is you choose to take this road through inspiration instead of being forced down this road because of desperation.

As a speaker and author who is also a singer/songwriter, I wrote a song a few years ago that has taken on a new meaning. The title of the song is "What Are They Leaving With?" It was written with my two daughters and two grandsons in mind. What seeds have I sown in their lives? What legacy will I leave for them?

I hate to say this, but I wasn't even thinking about an audience, keynote, reader or presentation when I wrote the song.

The song has taken on a new meaning. It is now also about my in-person and reading audiences. I am so humbled and grateful to be able to share the leadership and life lessons of great leaders and mentors in my life.

Even though I've given hundreds of presentations to thousands of attendees, I still prepare for each one. As I've prepared and as I write this book, I ask myself that question about my audience and readers; "What Are They Leaving With?"

As a thank you for reading this book, I would like you to listen and have a copy of the song. Visit GregLGilbert.com/Thanks for a free download. I hope you enjoy.

You should also ask yourself that question. The people you lead. The people you interact with. The people you love and care about. What are they leaving with after interacting with you? There are only a few possibilities; pain, pleasure, hatred, love or respect. You get to choose. I'll leave you with that.

Greg Gilbert

Thank You!

Thank you for your purchase and taking the time to read "The Power Of Better". Feel free to take advantage of the free leadership resources at GregLGilbert.com

As you read this book, you may be tempted to lay a copy on someone's desk with a Post-it note in certain chapters. Please don't do this. Give them a copy or recommended the book. None of us is perfect. We all have the potential to have an anonymous book show up with Post-it notes throughout.

Sign up for free updates on leadership lessons and how you can continue in the movement of "Getting Better".

Greg Gilbert is available for keynotes, breakout sessions and presentations at your next leadership meeting, conference or association meeting.

Visit GregLGilbert.com to receive a no-obligation quote for your next event.

About Greg Gilbert

If it pertains to Human Resources, leadership, management or supervision, Greg Gilbert has probably been there, done that, journaled it, heard the grievance and is now teaching and speaking about it.

He has utilized and witnessed the unbeatable benefit of Education, Engagement, Accountability and the Leader/Owner Mindset as a telephone repairman, Supervisor, Area Manager and as the primary HR contact for over 2000 team members. He began journaling "what worked" and "what failed" in 1978. That was the beginning of his presentations and ultimately, this book.

He is a firm believer in presentations with both content and humor. He sometimes utilizes "Mr. HR With A Guitar" as a unique method of sharing these lessons and adding humor. Thousands across the country have been introduced to "The Power Of Better" Movement through this "journey through his journal".

www.ingramcontent.com/pod-product-compliance
Lightning Source LLC
Chambersburg PA
CBHW020745180526
45163CB00001B/356